Spinning Inward

Spinning Inward

USING GUIDED IMAGERY WITH CHILDREN FOR LEARNING, CREATIVITY & RELAXATION

REVISED & EXPANDED EDITION

Maureen Murdock

SHAMBHALA
Boston & London
1987

For Brendan and Heather

SHAMBHALA PUBLICATIONS, INC.
Horticultural Hall
300 Massachusetts Avenue
Boston, Massachusetts 02115

9 8 7 6 5 4 3 2 1

First Edition
Printed in the United States of America

Distributed in the United States by Random House
and in Canada by Random House of Canada Ltd.

Library of Congress Cataloging-in-Publication Data

    Murdock, Maureen.
    Spinning inward.

    Bibliography: p.
    1. Imagery (Psychology) in children. 2. Learning, Psychology of.
3. Child development.   I. Title.
BF723.I47M87 1987   155.4'13   87-9740
ISBN 0–87773–422–4 (pbk.)

Contents

◎　◎　◎　◎　◎　◎　◎

Preface

The title *Spinning Inward* came to me as I looked at an exhibit of Salish Indian Spindle Whorls at the University of British Columbia Museum of Anthropology. As the Salish weaver spun the wool on the spindle whorl, the whorl became a blur. When it stopped, an image was revealed to the spinner. He would then carve this image into his spindle whorl. The essential act of imaging, like all creative art, is the bringing into being of a vision. The images we spin inwardly become the reality we spin out.

Acknowledgments

I'd like to express my thanks to all the children and teenagers with whom I have worked, and to those big children inside adult bodies who have assisted me in my teaching: Jill Mackay, Donna Wabnig, and Steve Tomasini. Special thanks go to my partners at the Center for Integrative Learning, with whom I spent thousands of hours from 1980 to 1984 imaging, developing new exercises, leading training sessions, waiting in airports, and eating ice cream: Anne Breutsch, Diane Battung, and Beverly-Colleen Galyean. Saul Arbess and Penny Joy were my partners in using guided imagery and video with Native American students in British Columbia; I am indebted to both of them for their flexibility, good humor, and dedication to the education of all children. My heartfelt thanks go to Dr. Paul Cummins, director of Crossroads School, Santa Monica, California, who had the foresight to know the value of imagery and gave me permission and support to explore these techniques in the classroom. Polly McVickar, my mentor at Pacific Oaks College, was a constant source of vision, encouraging me to see beyond immediate results.

Many of the exercises in this book have been inspired by the work of Deborah Rozman of the University of the Trees, my late partner, Beverly-Colleen Galyean, and Jean Houston, director of the Foundation for Mind Research in New York. I am deeply indebted to Dr. Houston for allowing and encouraging me to adapt her work for children and adolescents, particularly the Hero's Journey.

I have been encouraged in the last four years by the research of Dr. Howard Gardner of Harvard University, who has proposed a theory of multiple intelligences which include talents in linguistic, musical, logical-mathematical, spatial, bodily-kinesthetic, and personal skills. He advocates the education of interpersonal as well as intrapersonal intelligence, which is geared to helping the individual know who he or she is. Guided imagery is a well-researched tool for educating intrapersonal intelligence.

I offer deep personal thanks to my meditation partner, Midge Bowman, who has shared with me a vision for the education of the spirit. Other colleagues who have given me great moral support in my work are Flor Fernandez, Marti Glenn, Jeanette Jara, Carolyn Kenny, Shanja Kirstann, Steve Morgan, Betty Rothenberger, Sharyn McDonald, Jane Alexander Stewart, and Robin Van Doren. Kelvin Jones and Meibao Nee photographed my students and me, and Roberta Scotthorne shared pictures of students in British Columbia. Emily Sell and Kendra Crossen, my editors at Shambhala, gave me support and humor.

Special thanks to Siddhartha Olmedo, Drew Schaeffer, Heather Murdock, Laura Braverman, Jenny Belin, Sean Nordquist, Adam Hausmann, Jessica Yellin, Kevin Greenberg, Taro Joy, Jenny Reich, Christie Sanders, Heather Seineger, David Roberts, Alex Marshall, Erinn Berkson, Bekki Misiorowski, Andy Guss, and Matt Nasatir for their artwork and writing.

My husband, Lucien Wulsin, has been a constant source of support, good will, and love. I am particularly grateful for his patience, cooking, and back rubs during the writing of this book. My children, Heather and Brendan, first opened to me the world of children's imagery, and their images have been a constant source of magic and delight. In addition to that, they have taught me more than anyone about the unfolding mystery of human creativity, for which I am deeply grateful.

Special thanks also to my parents, Matthew and Julia Hennessey, and to Lucien Wulsin, Sr.

Spinning Inward

Introduction

◎　　◎　　◎　　◎　　◎　　◎　　◎

In August 1979 I had a powerful dream that seeded this book on the use of guided imagery with children and adolescents. From deep within myself I heard a wrenching primal groan and then felt the slow, painful growth of a redwood tree breaking ground at the center of my body. It continued upward until its branches came through the top of my head. At the base of its roots were two stone tablets inscribed with indecipherable hieroglyphics. I was quite shaken at first by the intensity of the dream, but it became clear to me that this dream heralded a work to do. For me the tablets signified the untouched recesses of the human mind.

For the last twenty years I have been fascinated as a parent, teacher, and learner with some very basic questions. How do we learn? How do we expand creativity? How do we know those things which we know intuitively?

In the mid-1970s I began to research the literature available on mind expansion and I began meditating. After several months of noticing the calming effects of meditation on myself, I introduced this technique to my own young children. Encouraged by their response, I then tried short centering exercises with my kindergarten class. The results amazed me; with a simple relaxation exercise at the beginning of the day, my pupils and I became calmer and more responsive to each other. My class showed an observable increase in attention span and creativity, developed better listening skills, and showed a new awareness of each other's feelings.

Inspired by these results, I studied the work of Jean Houston, Deborah Rozman, and George Leonard, who were advocating better integration of mind, body, and spirit. As I used some of their physical, mental, and spiritual imagery exercises in the third-grade class that I was then teaching, I observed that the children rapidly expanded their ability to learn and found a positive way to cope with the serious illness of one of their classmates.

In 1978 I wrote an article entitled "Meditation with Young Children," which was published by the *Journal of Transpersonal Psychology,* and received hundreds of letters from other parents and teachers who were using these techniques successfully in the United States, Europe, the Soviet Union, New Zealand, and the Philippines. Parents wrote about using imagery to relax their children and to unify their families. Students said they used imagery to calm themselves before a test. Teenagers asked for meditations to cope with a divorce in their family, a move to a new school, or finding new friends. Teachers reported better test scores as their students relaxed.

I continued to develop guided imagery exercises for my elementary classes and then started training other teachers, parents, and therapists in these techniques. Imagery exercises were used in the Los Angeles city schools from 1978 to 1981 in projects at Bell High and Main Street Elementary. In a pilot study using imagery exercises with Native American students I trained 1,500 teachers, children, and adolescents in these techniques throughout British Columbia in 1981. The results were documented in a special report by the Ministry of Education entitled *New Strategies in Indian Education: Utilizing the Indian Child's Advantage in the Elementary Classroom.*

In the first edition of this book (Culver City, Calif.: Peace Press, 1982), my primary focus was elementary school children, ages five to twelve. I have since had the opportunity to research the effectiveness of imagery with adolescents, and this book has been expanded to address the developmental stages of adolescence and how guided imagery serves as an effective tool to ease this transition from childhood to adulthood. I teach a human development course entitled "Mysteries" to junior high and twelfth-grade students at Crossroads School in Santa Monica, California. I have found the exercises to be effective at all age levels to calm, center, and expand consciousness.

This book is designed as a guidebook for using imagery at home and in the classroom or counseling setting. Do the exercises first yourself; return to the imagination and freedom you had as a child. When you are ready to guide others, you may wish either to read the exercises aloud or to tape-record them so that you may participate also. These exercises have been used on a one-to-one basis, with small groups, in typical classroom situations, and in large training sessions with up to two hundred adults.

Guided imagery is a process of going within, focusing attention on breath and bodily relaxation and moving to deeper levels of consciousness where more images are accessible to the conscious mind. This may take the form of a pleasant journey to the beach or mountains, a meeting with an inner figure of wisdom, or visualizing yourself as successful in whatever field of endeavor is your focus. Each time I lead an imagery exercise I learn something new about the infinite possibilities for learning, healing, and creativity with this technique.

A New Look at Our Children

❀ ❀ ❀ ❀ ❀ ❀ ❀

Our children are more intelligent than any previous generation. We used to think of the newborn child as an empty cup waiting to be filled with knowledge by its wise parents and all-knowing society. That theory no longer holds. Our grandparents knew what they were talking about when they observed that wisdom comes "out of the mouths of babes."

Our children know much more than we give them credit for. Their inherent knowledge is such that they see the present and the future more clearly than we do, and they are evolving at a much faster, more sophisticated rate than we did. For this reason, present learning techniques are inadequate for them.

It isn't enough for us to offer them stimulating learning environments; we must also reinforce what they already know. Hundreds of thousands of children *unlearn* what they know because we don't recognize their knowledge. They unlearn their own unique approach to learning new material because some teacher might think they are cheating if they remember too easily. Often adults speak of having erased their photographic memories as children because they didn't want their teachers to think they were learning too fast.

This book is about learning easily, creatively, and without stress. In this book we'll use imagery techniques as tools to help our children recognize what they already know, and to accelerate learning. These techniques are simple to use and require little time, no money, and no new materials. They travel where you travel. All you need to do is to recognize that we use imagery all of the time without realizing that we can put it to work for us.

WHAT IS IMAGERY?

Imagine what it would be like to sit by the sea right now, feeling a gentle salt breeze on your face and the warmth of the sun on your back. Listen to the roar of the surf as it meets the glistening wet sand.

Now, you may not have "seen" that picture, but you may have felt the sun's warmth or heard the waves rushing in. Think about it for a moment. How do you image? Do you *see* movies in your mind, *hear* symphonies, *smell* or *taste* words or ideas, or *feel* them in your body? You probably combine several of these forms.

Have you ever thought about actively using your images? Imagery is an extremely effective learning tool. We increase concentration and memory skills, improve academic learning, and excel in sports through the use of imagery. The use of positive, relaxing images helps us to reduce stress. Major university medical schools are researching the effectiveness of imagery in healing. Successful business people use imagery every day. Every good salesperson knows the power of positive imagery to increase sales.

Children think in images all of the time. They know things with all of their senses. But they lose this natural ability to learn with their sensory images unless we reinforce it. There are some interesting things that parents and educators should know about imagery, learning, and the brain.

LEARNING AND THE BRAIN

We learn more when we're relaxed. Information is more accessible to us when our brain waves are in a slower, larger pattern. When we shut out the distractions around us and focus on breath and muscle relaxation, our brain waves slow down.

You know that when you're relaxed and calm, ideas suddenly pop into your mind that solve problems you've spent hours trying to "figure out." As your body relaxes from the day's activities while lying in bed at night, you may suddenly have an insight that solves days of waking deliberation.

Albert Einstein, who had been considered an unsociable, dull student, discovered the theory of relativity in just this manner. One day, as he lay on his back playfully watching the sunlight as it came through his eyelashes, he wondered what it would be like to travel down a sunbeam. As he let his mind wander through that image, he had a sudden insight into exactly what it would be like. This creative insight enabled him to piece together the theory for which he became famous.

Einstein is said to have used both hemispheres of his brain simultaneously. His ideas came first as visual images, which he then translated into words and mathematical equations. He telegraphed this information back and forth between his hemispheres through the corpus callosum, the bundle of

6

TASKS PREFERRED BY LEFT HEMISPHERE	TASKS PREFERRED BY RIGHT HEMISPHERE
Time-oriented tasks:	Space-oriented tasks:
Doing first things first	Three-dimensional images
Step-by-step tasks	Patterns
Sequential analysis	Connections
Logic	Synthesizing tasks, whole view
Verbal tasks	Nonverbal tasks
Facts, lists, computation	Images, pictures, metaphors
	Dreams, insight, intuition

Source: Adapted from Betty Edwards, *Drawing on the Right Side of the Brain* (Los Angeles: J. P. Tarcher, 1979), p. 40.

nerve fibers that joins the two hemispheres of the brain. He has been quoted as saying that in his opinion the most important aspect of intelligence is the ability to use imagery with the information we know.[1] This is one way of putting whole-brain learning into practice.

Learning occurs throughout the entire brain. Recent brain research has given us the image of the brain in two halves: left and right. Each half *prefers* certain tasks. These tasks are not located *in* the brain; it is just that each hemisphere processes particular kinds of information. It is almost like a silent agreement between left and right on the coordination of tasks. The important thing to remember is that the whole brain is engaged in learning all of the time.

We are all familiar with the highly articulate, logical, analytic "left-brained" individual. We usually think of engineers, accountants, and lawyers when we think of such attributes. This person may attack a problem in step-by-step, logical fashion. A child with this learning style excels in school because our educational system is geared to verbal, written, and computational tasks and factual memory.

The "right-brained" individual is the aesthetic, synthetic, holistic thinker who excels in art, music, architecture, athletics, and other nonverbal pursuits. This individual approaches a problem in a holistic manner—that is, as a whole from start to finish, rather than step by step. He or she sees the "light at the end of the tunnel" but may not be able to tell you how to get there sequentially.

We can't really attribute these qualities to only the left or the right hemisphere, but we can say that schools have favored one type of learning: a verbal, linear, sequential, fact-oriented format. A child who does not learn in this way does not fit the format.

Dr. Michael Grady of the University of St. Louis points out some of the teaching and testing limitations of the current education system. "We are neglecting genius, which depends on both modes of hemispheric processing operating simultaneously by relying on left brain reading as the primary method of teaching and testing."[2] Using imagery followed by a verbal, written, or art task is one way of exercising the whole brain.

THE BRAIN AS A HOLOGRAM

Memory is not stored in only one part of the brain. We don't memorize facts and store them in one memory compartment. The research of Dr. Karl Pribram of Stanford University suggests that *memory is stored throughout the entire brain.*

Pribram compares the brain to a hologram. In vastly simplified terms, a hologram is a three-dimensional image of a picture projected in space. The image is stored on a photographic plate. Thousands of different images can be recorded on the same plate, and each of them can be reconstructed from any part of the plate. Even if the photographic plate is shattered, coherent light can be passed through one piece of it to reconstruct the entire three-dimensional image.

Pribram explains how the brain functions like a hologram. Millions of images are stored throughout the entire brain, and all memory is stored within each brain cell. If we have an image of the original conditions and context in which we learned something, we can remember it.[3]

This is not hard to understand if we think of recent research on DNA molecules. Biologists have found that the blueprint for a person's whole physical being is contained in the nucleus of every cell of the body, including hair cells and nail cells. If the master plan of our physical body is contained in each cell in our body, it seems natural that all memory is contained in each cell of our brain/body as well.

MULTISENSORY LEARNING

The implications of this theory of how the brain works are fascinating. It suggests that the image of every flower we have smelled, every touch we have felt, every sunset upon which we have gazed, is remembered throughout our brain. If we realize the role our senses play in learning, we can use our senses to bring these memories to the surface.

For instance, we may begin to associate a list of numbers that we wish to remember with the sounds or smells that we are aware of at the time we look at the numbers. Spelling words might be remembered by color association or how they feel. Learning won't be limited to rote memorization if we use our senses.

Most children have the natural ability to store memories by associating them with their senses. Kevin, one of my third-grade students, associated the "nine times" tables with the smell of pancakes. His father was cooking pancakes the morning Kevin learned his nines.

Children who learn in this manner usually lose this natural ability because it is discouraged or regarded as silly by their parents and teachers. If They are synesthetes (cross-sensors). Cross-sensing expands memory.

A famous example of sensory memory is that of "S," a newspaper reporter who was studied by the Russian psychologist A. R. Luria for his remarkable ability to remember details. Luria tested his memory in a variety of ways, including reading S a list of several hundred repetitive nonsense syllables, with no pattern to the sequence. Not only did S remember the full series, but he was able to repeat it in its entirety eight years later.

The response S gave was, "Yes, yes . . . this was a series you gave me once when we were in your apartment. You were sitting at the table and I at the rocking chair. You were wearing a gray suit, and you looked at me like this. . . . Now, then, I can see you saying . . ." and then he proceeded to reel off the series perfectly.

When he was given a random list of items to remember, S would spontaneously form a strong image of the item and associate it with some object along a road or street that he knew. He could recall the list of items by mentally walking down the street, seeing the objects he had associated with those items.[5]

One of my third-graders associated numbers with rhyming words. When she needed to recall a sum, she simply remembered her rhyming association. For example, "two plus two equals four" became a "blue double door."

Our children who learn in this manner usually lose this natural ability because it is discouraged or regarded as silly by their parents and teachers. If they do not learn in the manner in which the schools educate, they are ignored or labeled "learning-disabled." Through the use of guided imagery, parents and educators can both reinforce this natural ability to learn with the senses and improve our children's learning at school.

TWO

Using Imagery

Using imagery is like eating an artichoke. When we peel off the tough outer petals of the artichoke, we find the softer, more subtle inner petals and tasty core of the fruit. Imagery works in a similar way. The thick outer petals are like the high-level tensions that exist in our everyday environment. As we shut out the distractions of our hectic daily lives, we begin to find a wealth of creativity and wisdom within ourselves.

Guided imagery is a tool to unlock creativity. The exercises in *Spinning Inward* are not to be used as a therapeutic tool to deal with neurotic behavior or psychic phenomena. It is true that guided imagery is used in therapy by qualified clinicians, but that is not my aim in this book. I hope that these exercises will provide an opportunity for children and adults to experience together a fuller, more creative life.

You may wish to use the exercises in the order presented, or you may skip around the book, finding exercises that suit your particular needs. These exercises are not sequential; however, I suggest that you start with the Relaxation Exercise in Chapter 3 to begin the process.

GETTING COMFORTABLE

When I first began working with imagery, I spent several months doing breath and relaxation exercises before introducing them to my children. I used the relaxation exercise to center and calm myself during a particularly difficult emotional time in our family's life.

When I introduced the idea to my young children, then aged four and six, I told them that I was doing a fun exercise that helped me quiet down and listen to myself. I told Heather and Brendan that it was very much like daydreaming and that I believed that these exercises would help us learn more, be calmer, and have more fun. I asked them to try it with me, and we discussed a time that would suit everyone's needs. We chose the late afternoon to "play" with our images, and we called this time together "quiet time."

CHOOSING A TIME

AT HOME

The schedule of each family will dictate the best time to use imagery. Many families prefer the early morning before going to school and work. Some parents have told me that imagery exercises have replaced television in the evening, followed by storytelling that evolves from the images.

Some people use a short relaxation exercise before dinner so that each family member will be able to eat without tension and the frenzy that often characterizes family meals. Parents who are home when their children return from school often use imagery exercises to help their children settle down after a busy day.

IN THE CLASSROOM

Teachers use a short relaxation exercise in the beginning of the day, after lunch, before certain classes, or before tests. Consistency is the key. Finding a consistent time each day or once a week establishes continuity for you and the children. This time becomes one that the children look forward to. And you don't need a lot of time; five minutes are enough to start, and you'll increase the time naturally as you explore the process.

In my third-grade classroom, the scenario went something like this.

It's 8:55 A.M. and I turn off the lights in the classroom. Most of the children stop midmovement or midsentence. A few card sharks playing a game of War in the pillowed book corner continue in hushed tones. The doves coo in their cage. We hear the sound of dominoes toppling one by one in the intricate pattern created by Tim. I turn the lights back on, and the children complete the words or sentences on the tips of their tongues. They put away their games or marking pens, hang up their sweaters, and slowly assemble on the rug.

Seated on the rug, all twenty-eight of us form two concentric circles. I wait until everyone is settled. "Why don't you hang up your jacket, John? I think you'd be more comfortable. . . . Alan, do you think you'll be able to sit next to Joe without wanting to talk to him? . . . Oh, Marissa, you're back in class! How was your trip?" After a couple of minutes of squirming and yawning, the children and I come to rest and begin our daily quiet time.

"Find a position that you can maintain for several minutes, and close your eyes. Focus your attention on your breath. That's right, just relax, and

be aware of letting go of the tension in the muscles in your body with each breath you take. Breathe in . . . and . . . out . . . in . . . and . . . out."

WHAT'S THE BEST ENVIRONMENT?

AT HOME

Find a place in the house or outside that is free from distraction. Unplug the phone, and make it clear to friendly neighbors that you are busy. A creative sign that says GENIUS AT PLAY—DO NOT DISTURB might just do the trick.

You may wish to set up an environment that is reserved for this time together with pillows or mats and plants. Make it beautiful. Some people have told me that each of their family members brings his or her quiet-time pillow to the living room or family room when it is time to begin. This signals, with a minimum of talk and directions, that the process is about to start.

One of my students made a "meditation room" in her closet. She cleaned out the shoes in the bottom of her closet and filled it with soft blue pillows. She then invited her mother in every evening to lead her through the imagery exercise that we had done that day in class. These exercises helped her mother through a very painful divorce.

12

IN THE CLASSROOM

If you have a rug area in the room, your class could sit in a circle or two concentric circles. Older children sit at their desks with their heads down, or they simply close their eyes or look at the floor. A prearranged signal to start your imagery exercise is helpful. I turned off the lights. Soothing music, the sound of a gong or bell, and lighting a candle have all been used by other teachers with success.

YOUR FRAME OF MIND

It is best to work with imagery when you are fairly relaxed. Trying to lead an imagery exercise when you are angry or upset will probably interfere with the process. Some families and classes actually use relaxation exercises before trying to settle a dispute. They find that their solutions are then more flexible and creative.

These exercises are enjoyable. You and your children are sharing parts of yourselves that you don't ordinarily show to others, so you may find yourselves becoming closer. You may discover that quiet time becomes an opportunity to share your wishes, dreams, and fears with each other.

RESISTANCE TO USING IMAGERY

AT HOME

You may receive resistance from some family members, but don't be deterred. Explain to your reluctant child or spouse that you would like to try these exercises to help all of you relax, learn more easily, improve memory skills, get along better, and be more creative and productive. It's hard to argue against objectives like these!

Work with those family members who wish to join. The others will include themselves when they are ready. Make it very clear, however, that they may not interfere or make noise (especially by watching television) when the rest of the family is having their quiet time together. Perhaps they could read a book, listen to soothing music, or draw while you're involved with imagery.

You may also find that age affects how much a child wishes to participate. When my children were younger, they were eager to join me. As they became adolescents, other interests took priority. During high school my son often requested a brain exercise before a major test to help him relax and improve memory. At age seventeen my daughter preferred to relax and create by listening to music and painting. Each individual's needs and mode of expression should be honored and respected.

IN THE CLASSROOM

Even though visualization and imagery techniques have gained widespread acceptance and use in sports, health care, and business, many students have not been exposed to these teaching tools in the classroom. Explain to your students and their parents that the purpose of these exercises is to reduce stress, increase learning, and improve memory skills. Emphasize that attention is prerequisite to listening and learning, and that imagery helps the student to focus and attend. I always tell my students that this is a tool I value in my personal life to stay calm and centered.

I suggest to my students that they close their eyes or look down at the floor with "soft" or half-closed eyes. I state two rules before we begin: no talking or whispering during the exercise and no interfering with anyone else. I understand that because of the unfamiliarity of the technique not all students will participate at first, but they all must learn to respect others' choice to relax and focus.

It may take several weeks before teacher and students become comfortable with the process. I advise teachers to give themselves six weeks before expecting positive results. Expect giggling at first. Students may be embarrassed, be worried about others looking at them, or view the idea of having time in school to exercise their brain as silly. I find that the giggling disappears if students receive no attention for it.

The most surprising thing to me is that students themselves ask those who are disruptive to stop. They don't want their imagery time interrupted. When I taught third grade, my students asked latecomers to wait outside the classroom until our quiet time was over. Before long there were no latecomers!

Sometimes there is resistance from the parents of students. In my class, some parents were skeptical at first, so I invited them to join our morning quiet time. Without exception they enjoyed it, and several parents made it a regular part of their day to join us for quiet time when they brought their child to school. They enjoyed beginning their work or other daily activities relaxed and centered.

One parent said that her child complained about closing her eyes. It scared her. I suggested that she keep her eyes open, and that alleviated the fear.

One third-grade boy and his mother requested that he not be included in the exercises. He thought they were "dumb," but he liked to hear what his classmates had to say. I gave him the choice of joining us on the rug and listening, or sitting and reading in the reading corner. Most of the time he sat just on the outside of the circle, listening to the images described by the other children.

FOLLOW-UP

After a guided imagery exercise some children like to discuss how their body felt or what images occurred to them. Others prefer to draw or paint the images that emerged, write about them, or express them in movement. Go slowly at first and respect everyone's timing. Children are much closer to their inner images than we adults are. Allow them their own time to reveal their experiences to you. You can't force an orchid to bloom; you can, however, delight in the process of unfolding.

TRUST THE PROCESS

One thing I have learned from years of using imagery exercises with both children and adults is to have no set expectations of how and when people will respond. I do, however, have full trust that this process has great value to those who avail themselves of it. Find the exercises that work for you and your children; improvise; invent new ones. Give full range to your imagination.

You may find that sitting is ineffective for you and a hyperactive child. You may wish to stand up or lie down. Many parents and teachers hold young children in their laps and gently rub their backs while leading a relaxation exercise. This has a soothing, quieting effect. Another suggestion is to give the child a small ball of clay to hold while doing the exercise. This is particularly helpful with kinesthetic learners.

Older students and adults may fall asleep if lying down while doing imagery exercises, and snoring can be quite disruptive to the class! You might suggest that they sit up in a comfortable position with their back supported by the wall or a chair. Some children and adults prefer to move while working with imagery. One man moves his hands constantly during the process, drawing in the air the images that he sees in his mind. He is an engineer and inventor and uses imagery to activate his fertile imagination.

A few physical stretching exercises prior to guided imagery may prime the body and mind for more vivid images. Some of the simple exercises demonstrated in *Awareness through Movement* by Moshe Feldenkrais are excellent for getting the whole body/mind system in harmony. *Listening to the Body* by Robert Masters and Jean Houston is also an excellent resource.

16

THREE

Tuning In Your Own Station

The prepared or one-pointed mind is open to creative insight because it bypasses thinking.

Joseph Chilton Pearce
Magical Child

ATTENTION

Possibly one of the most valuable things we can teach our children is how to attend. How to be in attention, how to be aware of the conscious existence of ourselves as human beings. How to be fully present in mind and body at each moment.

Teaching children attention to their breath and suggesting ways to relax their bodies enable them to quiet or calm their emotions. Thus they gain fuller understanding of themselves.

The word *attention* comes from the Latin *attendere,* "to stretch forward." What do we wish our children to stretch toward? The values they see mirrored around them in our competitive, stressful, consumption-oriented society? Or a clear sense of who they *are?*

Our lifestyles are so full of what we *do* that we have little time to simply *be.* Our fast-paced, time-segmented daily lives make it difficult to be fully present at any one moment; we're always thinking about what's going to happen next. There is no time for quiet or reflection.

In an exercise that I once did with my third-grade class on what they didn't like in their lives, the symbol that appeared in all of their drawings was a ticking alarm clock. When I asked them to elaborate about the clock, typical responses were "I hate rushing from school to soccer practice," "I never have any time to just sit," "I don't get enough time to play with my friends because my mom has to pick me up early so she can go someplace else." In a similar exercise with older students, one commented: "I thought

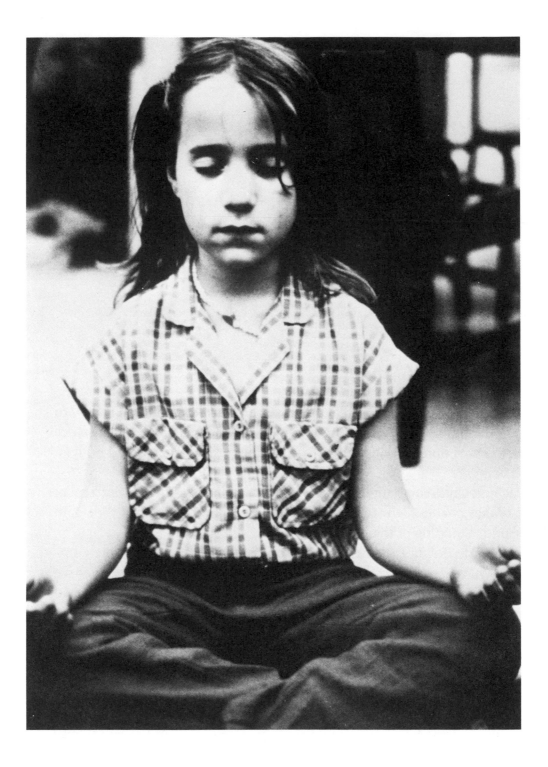

teachers would let up on the work during senior year, but we have more than ever. I have no time for my friends."

Short imagery exercises help a child tune out the distractions and demands of everyday life and to focus on *being*.

> Close your eyes and sit very quietly. Now just listen to your breath. Breathe in . . . and . . . out. In . . . and . . . out. Now continue breathing in this manner, letting go of any thoughts, feelings, and worries you might have at this time. Just listen to your breath as you breathe gently in . . . and . . . out . . . in . . . and . . . out. Notice the air moving in and out of your nostrils.

In this exercise the attention is focused on *one* thing: the calm, quiet rhythm of something we normally do with no awareness—breathing.

RELAXATION

Once you've mastered this simple exercise, you may wish to take it one step further and attend to relaxing your body. Notice how your body feels at this very moment. Are you aware of carrying any tension in your back or neck? Are you holding your breath while you read? Many people hold their breath while they concentrate, often incurring headaches.

Relaxation Exercise

AGE: 3 through adult
TIME: 5 minutes

Find a comfortable spot in which to sit or lie down, and lead your child, family, or class through this exercise.

Close your eyes and sit (or lie down) very quietly. Take a couple of moments and notice how your body feels. Are you holding your breath, or do you breathe evenly? Notice if you feel any tension or stress in any part of your body. Now you're going to relax your body as you relax your breath.

Breathe in . . . and . . . out . . . and . . . in . . . and . . . out, and allow yourself to let go of any thoughts or worries. Gently continue to breathe in . . . and . . . out . . . and focus your attention on your feet. Just notice your feet, nothing else. Notice how they feel. It may be the first time that you have put all of your attention on your feet. Now, as you take a deep breath, tense or squeeze the muscles in your feet . . . hold it . . . and now release the tension in the muscles of your feet as you breathe out. And now continue breathing gently and calmly. (*Pause*)

Now focus your attention on your legs—just your legs, nothing else— and notice how they feel. Now breathe in as you squeeze the muscles in your legs . . . hold it . . . and now release the tension in your legs as you breathe out. (*Pause*)

Now focus your attention on your bottom and pelvic area. Breathe in as you squeeze the muscles in your bottom and pelvis . . . hold it . . . and release the tension in your bottom and pelvis as you breathe out. (*Pause*)

Focus your attention on your back . . . breathe as you squeeze your back . . . hold it . . . and now release the tension in your back as you breathe out. (*Pause*)

Focus your attention on your abdomen . . . just notice how it feels . . . notice whether you pull in the muscles in your abdomen. Now gently breathe in as you squeeze the muscles in your abdomen . . . hold it . . . and relax. (*Pause*)

Focus your attention on your chest . . . hold it . . . and now relax. And just continue to breathe gently and calmly. Focus your attention on your shoulders. . . . Notice if you carry more tension in one shoulder than another. Now breathe in as you squeeze the muscles in your shoulders . . . hold it . . . and relax. (*Pause*)

Now focus on your arms and hands, and when you squeeze the muscles in your hands, actually make a fist with your fingers, and then very slowly open your fingers when you release the tension. Breathe in as you squeeze the muscles in your arms and hands . . . hold it . . . and relax. (*Pause*)

Now focus your attention on your jaw and facial muscles, noticing how they feel. Breathe in as you squeeze the muscles in your jaw and eyes, nose and mouth . . . hold it . . . and now relax, letting go of any tension that you may carry in your jaw and facial muscles. (*Pause*)

Now focus your attention on your forehead and your head. Breathe in as you squeeze the muscles in your forehead and head . . . hold it . . . and relax. And now focus your attention on your breath . . . breathing gently and calmly . . . and enjoy the relaxation of your body.

(*After a minute*) Now bring yourself back to full waking consciousness as I count to three. Open your eyes at the count of three. One . . . two . . . three.

As you focus attention on breath, on each muscle group, on each part of the body, you are learning how to focus attention. The more I used short relaxation exercises in the early morning with my children, the more convinced I became that these simple exercises helped us to concentrate. And we need to concentrate to learn.

EXERCISE 2
Waterfall of White Light

AGE: 5 through adult
TIME: 5 minutes

Close your eyes and begin to focus your attention on your breath. Give your-self the suggestion that with each exhalation your body becomes more and more relaxed. Now imagine that a beautiful waterfall of white light is enter-ing the top of your head. You feel its gentle healing energy throughout your brain and pouring over your face, your chin, and your neck. The waterfall of white light now continues to move into your chest and shoulders and back. It moves down your arms and hands and out through your fingertips, taking with it any stress that you have held in your body. The white light continues to flow into your abdomen and solar plexus, your pelvis and but-tocks. It continues moving down into your thighs, knees, and calves. Now it enters your ankles and feet and goes out through your toes, taking with it any stress or discomfort that you have stored in your body. Now you are in a continuous waterfall of white light. Every part of your being is filled with white light. Allow this energy to wash over you, and enjoy the gentle calm it brings. (*Pause 1 minute*) Now slowly bring yourself back to full waking consciousness. I will count to ten. Join me counting aloud at six, and open your eyes at ten, feeling relaxed and alert. One . . . two . . . three . . . four . . . five . . . six . . . seven . . . eight . . . nine . . . ten.

RESPONSES TO WATERFALL EXERCISE

The waterfall came down and splashed up and down and it kept going over and over from my head to my toes.
　　　　　　　　　　　　　　　　　　　—*Heather, age five*

The waterfall of white light made me feel warm and tingly. I felt peaceful.—*Sid, age eight*

22

FOUR

Learning with All the Senses

@ @ @ @ @ @ @

LEARNING WITH THE FIVE SENSES

When you imagine a scene, do you see, hear, feel, taste, or smell the image? If I ask you to remember a time when you first tasted apple pie, do you see yourself as a child sitting in your grandmother's or mother's kitchen? Do you hear the sound of family members around you? Perhaps you experience the texture of the warm apples in your mouth, or salivate as you smell and taste the tartness of the apples and the delicate crust. You may observe that you experience a combination of several of these sensations. Most of us do. We don't just experience one sensation. We're much more interesting.

Just as we *sense* in multiple ways, we also *learn* in multiple ways. Some of us respond primarily auditorily, to sounds and the spoken word. Some need to see a visual diagram or picture to understand an idea. And yet others know things with their bodies. They learn kinesthetically, with a felt or muscular sensation. The idea "moves" for them.

We may think of ourselves as being verbally/auditorily oriented, visually oriented, or kinesthetically oriented, but we are probably using all of these systems simultaneously. In some instances, however, we are aware of one system more than another.[1]

I know that when I listen to a lecture I have to convert the words I hear into a visual outline or diagram to understand fully what I have heard. A close friend of mine stands at the back of the lecture hall so that she can move while the lecturer speaks. She understands more fully when she moves her body.

A former third-grade student of mine named Tony could never sit still while I demonstrated a lesson on the chalkboard. He had to poke the child sitting next to him or rock back and forth in his chair, distracting both me and the rest of the class. After changing his seat to various locations in the classroom without success, I tried a new tactic.

I asked Tony if he would sponge off the art/clay table while I presented a phonics lesson to the class. I had a sense that he needed to move in order to listen fully. While he sponged in a circular motion, I noticed that he was paying very close attention to what I was saying.

After the lesson I quizzed the class about the rules I had presented for vowel blends, and Tony got a perfect score of 10. He had never received a score higher than 3 before. To me, it was obvious that he learned as he moved. For some reason, it was easier for him to *hear* what I was saying and to understand the lesson I wrote on the chalkboard if he was *moving* his body.

Working with imagery exercises, I began to notice children's learning styles. Matt said that he "*saw*" four fields filled with blue and yellow flowers, which formed two squares. This was interesting to me because Matt was having difficulty following *oral* instructions but had no difficulty if the directions were *written* on the board. He loved mapmaking and art. Perhaps he needed *visual* cues to understand a concept, and that was why he had so much difficulty with verbal/oral tasks like taking dictation or entering into group discussions.

Liza said she "*felt* the bark of a tree" and then *felt* like she was running up a hill. When she communicated an idea to me or to the class, she expressed it with her whole body: arms waving, head tilting, and feet dancing. She actually *moved* through an idea.

Some children primarily image visually. Others *hear* images. I remember asking my daughter, Heather, where she got the ideas for the elaborate dialogue in one of her stories. "Oh, I just hear the people talking, and I write it down." Many children are aware that their senses of smell and taste elicit memories. What's your first memory associated with hot apple pie?

LEARNING WITH THE KINESTHETIC SENSE

Probably the most predominant of the image senses for children is the kinesthetic or *body* sense. Your child can imagine running, swimming, or doing gymnastics and naturally make use of this ability to improve athletic skills.

A parent recently asked me what a kinesthetic image was and how her daughter, Jessica, had learned to ride her bicycle so quickly. I explained to her that the kinesthetic image is our *imagined muscular sense of our body* and that we can use this image of our body to learn. She told me that Jessica had tried out her new bicycle, had fallen, and had told her parents she needed "to teach her kinesthetic body to ride the bike perfectly." She then sat down in the alley, closed her eyes, and imagined herself riding her bicycle perfectly.

"It was amazing," her mother said. "I actually saw her body come into alignment. She got up, got on the bike, and began to ride it. She was a bit wobbly at first, but she never fell. She was so happy with herself!"

The kinesthetic sense can be used to improve academic skills as well. I once asked my third-grade class how they memorized their multiplication tables. They looked at me quizzically. I then asked them if they used rhythms. Again, blank stares. I then sang as I tapped my thigh: "Sev-en times sev-en is for-ty-nine." Immediately 70 percent of the class started clapping, tapping, and snapping various multiplication facts. Many demonstrated their syllabification of words by chanting and thigh slapping and told me that this is the way they "beat out" their spelling words. How many children are told to stop tapping their pencils during a test or to sit still and pay attention, even though their natural way of learning may be to move?

The movement and inner rhythm of my own son drove me to distraction when he was in the fourth grade. Upstairs in his room Brendan "studied" vocabulary words while drumming on his books, tapping his feet on the rungs of his chair, rocking back and forth, and punctuating each beat with hoots and hollers. He sounded like a one-boy percussion band, and it felt like 5.6 on the Richter scale! He consistently got perfect scores in spelling tests and told me that drumming was his method of memorizing. This method is admittedly hard on the nerves of other family members but is one shared by many children.

Children are not the only ones who move when learning. Adults "pace" through the solution to problems or have insights into complex business strategies during early-morning jogs. A highly gifted high school teacher recently told me that she does her lesson plans for an entire week while playing golf on Sunday morning. A video filmmaker says that he sees with his whole body; he knows a scene is right when he "feels" it with his body.

How can we reinforce these different ways of knowing so that we can encourage our children's natural learning abilities rather than discourage or stifle them? One way is to begin to notice how your child learns. Ask him or her, and listen to the answer with all of your senses.

NOTE TO PARENTS

Exercise 3 is a wonderful way to stimulate creative writing or an art activity. When your child recounts his or her adventure on the cloud, a story may emerge that could involve the whole family. You may find it useful and fun to tape the response if your child is not comfortable writing it. Taping is an excellent tool to record ideas for use in subsequent stories. You may then wish to write it or type it as a caption to your child's illustration.

NOTE TO TEACHERS

In addition to being a tool to stimulate creative writing and art expression, this exercise alerts you to the primary sensing modes of the children. It also helps you to teach them about their senses and to encourage sensory imagery in writing and poetry.

EXERCISE 3

Multisensory Imagery

AGE: 8 through adult
EXERCISE: 5–10 minutes
FOLLOW-UP: 10–15 minutes

In the following imagery exercise, several sensory images are suggested to both sides of the brain.[2] These include images of seeing, hearing, taste, smell, and the kinesthetic sense. It is an exercise to make children more aware of their senses.

Sit in a comfortable position. Close your eyes and focus your attention on your breathing. (*Pause*)

As you breathe at a relaxed rate, you let go of any tension in your body, feeling more and more relaxed. (*Pause*)

Now focus your attention on your brain, and imagine that it is a wonderful, smooth waterslide and that you are sliding down all of the runs . . . up and down all the convolutions of your brain. (*Pause*)

Now let that image go. In a moment I will suggest to you several images on each side of your brain. Keep your eyes closed, and look to the left side of your brain. On the left side you experience the color blue. (*Pause*)

Now let the image go, and look up into the right side of your brain. On the right side you experience the color orange. Now let that image go, and on the left you experience red . . . and on the right green. On the left you experience a skier swiftly coming down a slope . . . on the right a child is swinging back and forth on a swing. . . . On the left you feel the texture of soft red velvet . . . on the right the texture of tree bark. On the left you feel the skin of a newborn baby . . . on the right you feel the texture of fine sandpaper. On the left you smell pancakes cooking . . . on the right the scent of a pine tree. On the left you taste a cold lime Popsicle. On the right you hold a juicy lemon in your hand. You cut out a slice from the lemon and touch just the tip of your tongue to the inside of the lemon. On the left you taste a sour pickle . . . on the right you taste a firm ripe banana. . . . On the left you hear the soft tinkling of wind chimes. . . . On the right you hear a loud bus horn. On the left you hear your first name . . . on the right you hear your last name. On the left you hear a kitty meow, and on the right you hear the purr of a cat.

27

Now let those images go, and imagine that your body is as light as a feather. And you imagine that a soft, fluffy cloud comes along and picks up your imaginary or kinesthetic body. And this cloud will take you anywhere you wish to go on an adventure. It will gently sit you down, and when you are ready to return, the cloud will bring you back here into your physical body. Now you have a minute of clock time equal to all the time that you need to have an adventure on your cloud. After the minute you will hear my voice calling you back. (*Pause 1 minute*)

Now it's time to return. Your cloud picks you up and brings you back here and gently sets you down in your physical body. And you become aware of your physical body. . . . In a moment I will count to ten. Join me at the count of six, opening your eyes at ten, feeling fully alert, more relaxed, and with an extended sensory system. One . . . two . . . three . . . four . . . five . . . six . . . seven . . . eight . . . nine . . . ten.

In Exercise 3 and in many of the exercises that follow, I use the phrase coined by Dr. Jean Houston, "You now have one (or two or three) minute(s) of clock time equal to all of the time you need." During an imagery exercise the child experiences "subjective time." The brain processes millions of images in microseconds, so in one sixty-second period children *do* have all the time they need to complete the imagery. Knowing that, they do not have to worry about when the exercise will end; that's up to you.

After a minute, or whatever time frame you have suggested, slowly suggest that it is time to come back to full waking consciousness. This gives the children time to complete their image. Then suggest awareness of body, face, and hands so the children will feel firmly grounded and alert when you end the exercise. Asking the children to join you at the count of six further increases their sense of awareness and alertness.

RESPONSES TO MULTISENSORY IMAGERY

When I heard my last name it echoed. I also heard the wind chimes. And when I was sliding I was on the left side of my brain.—*Adam, age nine*

I could see all of the images; I just couldn't feel the velvet. We went through a time door to the sky, and there were rides all around.—*Jenny, age seven*

I found myself out in space on the cloud and I went back in time to before the earth was—to when the whole universe was just a

I am floting in a brain I see a race car and a strawberry. I see numbers and letters. Then my specil cloud picks me up and takes me to the baby Animal Farm and I am the only one there exsept for the feeder. And she said that know one ever comes to see the animals so I could take one home to keep for a pet if I take care of it and feed the right food. So I took home the baby elefant and feed and keep reel nice.

HEATHER

speck of dust. And when I got out in space I flew around with a space pack on my back. When I came back to the classroom I came forward in time, so it started with the speck of dust and then I saw specks of the earth and then I saw dinosaurs on the earth, then cities. It was really neat, and then I came back here.

—*Brooke, age eight*

After doing Exercise 4, discuss with your children the link between memory and senses. Do they remember multiplication tables or spelling words by taste, smell, color, or movement? Some people find, to their great surprise, that they can "see" an entire page that they were studying if they smell the scent of the flowers present in the room while they were studying. Or a complex math formula may be recalled by its thorny texture! Have fun with the associations.

EXERCISE 4

Crossing Senses

AGE: 7 through adult
EXERCISE: 5–10 minutes
FOLLOW-UP: 10–15 minutes

Lie down or sit in a position that you can maintain for a while. Close your eyes and focus your attention on your breath. Breathe in . . . and . . . out . . . in . . . and . . . out . . . as your body becomes more and more relaxed. In a moment you will hear some music ["Spring" from Vivaldi's *The Four Seasons*], and you will listen to the music with your toes as you actually breathe the music in through your toes. Now you breathe the music in through your fingertips. Feel the music with your eyes, nose, and mouth . . . and now feel it with every hair on your body. (*Pause 1 minute*)

And now you begin to experience the taste of the music, soft and gentle on your tongue. You smell the music, and before you beautiful colors and images of this music unfold. (*Pause*)

You find yourself skiing down a long, snowy slope to the music, and you feel the sound of the snow. (*Pause*)

Imagine yourself dancing to the sounds of soft blue velvet and smell the aroma of an ice cube. Taste a daisy and see the texture of coarse sandpaper. You move gracefully through strawberry Jell-O and tiptoe through honey. You hear a gooey roasted marshmallow and taste the lowest note on the tuba. Feel the sound of children's laughter and hear the touch of a kitten's fur. You taste your favorite childhood treat and spend a minute of clock time equal to all of the time you need smelling, tasting, hearing, moving, and seeing the images of a favorite time in your life. Begin.

(*After a minute*) It is now time to bring yourself back to full waking consciousness. Become very aware of your body as I count from one to ten. Please join me in counting aloud at the count of six, opening your eyes at ten. You will feel alert and be more conscious of your senses. One . . . two . . . three . . . four . . . five . . . six . . . seven . . . eight . . . nine . . . ten.

RESPONSES TO CROSSING SENSES

When you said feel the music through your toes, it felt tingly and cold. In my chest it felt like little men dancing. When I

sensed it through my fingertips it got smoother and smoother. It tasted like chap stick and smelled like bubble gum.
                                                        —*Devin, age eight*

It didn't taste like anything but it smelled like little notes floating in the air. It felt rough.—*Shelly, age nine*

It tasted like chocolate ice cream and smelled like a rose. It looked like I was riding a bike and running at the same time.
                                                        —*Jay, age eight*

I listened to the music and I really couldn't do all the things that you asked us to do.—*Derek, age eight*

It is important to recognize that the last comment is a common response when first working with guided imagery. Many children say that they don't "see" anything at first. My usual reply is to ask them how they felt during the exercise. They may say "relaxed" or "quiet," and I tell them that that is enough. They don't have to see, hear, taste, smell, or feel images, but the images may become more vivid as they practice these exercises. The imagery muscle is just like any other muscle; it has to be exercised to work!

You may wish to precede Exercise 5 with a discussion about the five senses and how we use them every day. Each room of perception can be viewed as a single complete exercise, or you may wish to go through all the rooms of perception as a complete exercise. If working with a preschool-age child, do one room of perception at a time. Follow up this imagery exercise with a discussion of your child's experience, or suggest that your child draw, write, or act out his or her images.

Because of the length of this exercise, you may wish to clean one room of perception a day. This is an excellent exercise to use before a poetry assignment, especially if you emphasize sensory description. The room of the sixth sense usually generates a good discussion about experiences of *déjà vu*. This exercise is an effective tool to stimulate creative writing in students aged twelve through eighteen.

EXERCISE 5

The House of Perception

AGE: 3 through adult
EXERCISE: 5–15 minutes
FOLLOW-UP: 10–30 minutes

In this exercise imagine going into the "room" of each sense—sight, hearing, smell, taste, and touch—and cleaning out any cobwebs in each imaginary room that may be preventing you from perceiving each sense clearly.[3]

Close your eyes and follow your breath in . . . and . . . out . . . of your nostrils. Allow your body to become very relaxed and quiet as you breathe in . . . and . . . out. Now imagine that you are walking down a street and you see a very interesting house: this is the house of perception, the house of your senses, and as you walk into the house you see that there are many rooms with doors with symbols on them.

The first room you come to has a large eye on the door. You open the door and realize that this is the room of vision. It is filled with junk, the garbage that you have put there over the years to prevent you from seeing as clearly as you might. In your mind's eye, see all the junk and cobwebs in the room, and begin to clean out the room of vision with cleansers, a broom, a vacuum—whatever you need. If you wish to, actually go through the cleaning motions with your body, knowing that as you do so, you are improving your vision. (*Pause 1 minute*)

When you are finished, you throw out all the junk and you open the windows and let the room fill with fresh air. See it bright and shining. Look out the window and see the scene outside, noticing all of the colors. (*Pause 30 seconds*)

Now it is time to leave the room of vision.

At this time you can suggest that your children either proceed to the room of hearing or slowly open their eyes and notice the colors around them. Suggest that they write, draw, or tell about what they have experienced in the room of vision.

Proceed now to the room of hearing. It has a big ear on the door. As you open the door, you hear a cacophony of discordant sounds. The room is filled with rubbish. There is a lot of wool on the walls and a thick covering of wax all over the place. Clean up the room of hearing, making it as clean as you can, knowing that you are improving your quality of hearing. (*Pause*)

When you finish with this cleaning, open the windows and let some fresh air swoosh in. Hear it swoosh in. Listen to the breeze as it whispers past you. (*Pause*)

Now listen closely to all the sounds around you. (*Pause 30 seconds*) Listen to your breath. (*Pause*) And now it's time to leave the room of hearing.

Proceed now to the room of smell. You know the room of smell because there is a large nose on the door. As you open the door, you smell a combination of terrible scents, including old moldy food. Begin to clean the room of smell, really scrubbing all the corners and cracks in the room. Again, you may wish to go through the movements of cleaning and scrubbing. (*Pause one minute*)

Make it light and clean and sweet-smelling. As you do so, you begin to smell all of your favorite scents. (*Pause*) Enjoy this room now, breathing in its fragrance deeply. (*Pause 30 seconds*) Now it's time to leave the room of smell.

Proceed now to the room of taste. This room has a large tongue on the door. This room is very disorderly. All of the foods are mixed up, and you begin to taste your least favorite foods: liver, spinach, Brussels sprouts. As you clean the room of taste, be sure to sort out all of the different tastes, separating the peanut butter from the pizza, the apples from the oranges. (*Pause 30 seconds*)

Now that you've cleaned and arranged the room of taste, you begin to taste some of your favorite foods. (*Pause 1 minute*) It is now time to leave the room of taste.

Proceed now to the room of touch, which has a large hand on the door. Clean it up very thoroughly, throwing out all the junk that prevents you from feeling textures. (*Pause*)

When you've finished cleaning, move about the room and slowly touch the textured walls. Rub your hands over the wallpaper, which is a mixture of velvet, silk, sandpaper, satin, ice, and tree bark, and notice how good everything feels to your skin. (*Pause 30 seconds*)

Now physically begin to rub your hands on your clothes, noticing the texture of your clothes, and then gently feel your face and hair. (*Pause*) Notice how wonderful you feel. (*Pause*)

It is now time to leave the room of touch, and when you open your eyes you may wish to touch the textures around you.

There is one more room to clean, and this room is the attic. You walk up an old spiral staircase to the attic, which is full of cobwebs and bats. This is the room of your sixth sense . . . the room of extrasensory perception . . . the room of inner vision. And it is very dusty because it has not been used for a long time. You begin to clean the room of the sixth sense, and you notice a circular window at the far end of the room. It is so dirty that you cannot see out of it. You begin to scrape and wash it clean, and as you do so, a beautiful scene unfolds for you. (*Pause 1 minute*)

As you continue to look out this circular window, you notice all the colors, sounds, smells, tastes, and textures about this scene. (*Pause 30 seconds*)

It is now time to leave the room of the sixth sense. You close the door, walk down the spiral staircase . . . past the rooms of your five senses, and you leave your cleaning materials in the hall closet. You leave the house of perception and find yourself sitting here. As you slowly open your eyes, become aware of all the colors, sounds, smells, textures, and tastes around you.

RESPONSES TO "THE HOUSE OF PERCEPTION"

ROOM OF VISION

My room of vision was like a triangle and all the cobwebs were in the corner. When I opened my eyes the colors were fuzzy because the lights were out. But when the lights went on the colors popped out at me. Books were on the floor, puzzle pieces were on the floor. I cleaned up the windows and when I looked at the room the room was shining. When I put the puzzle pieces together, they were two eyes, and they were my eyes, and they were shining.—*Carlos*

ROOM OF HEARING

My door was like an ear. Inside there were these high-pitched, screeching sounds. I cleaned out all of the wax. My ear begin to hurt because I was scrubbing too hard.—*Chris*

ROOM OF SMELL

After cleaning the room of the smelling sense I smelled rose and cooked chicken. I smelled or it seemed like my nose was smelling something furry, as if my cat was rubbing against my nose.

—*Carlos*

ROOM OF TOUCH

It was hard for me but then I saw two hands opening up and I went in and felt soft textures.—*David*

ROOM OF TASTE

At first it was awful, full of mold and foods I don't like, and then I cleaned it and tasted pizza and Coke.—*Devin*

ROOM OF THE SIXTH SENSE

I started to clean the window of the sixth sense from the middle outward and it was like drawing the mandala. When I looked out the window I saw the ocean and growing on top of the ocean were a whole bunch of flowers.—*Janine*

Verbal versus Nonverbal Learning

@ @ @ @ @ @ @

VISUAL AND KINESTHETIC LEARNERS

Many children are denied the opportunity to use their full learning potential by current educational techniques. Budget cutbacks affecting the arts and physical education not only eliminate enrichment classes, but may actually eliminate classes that help visual or kinesthetic learners learn. Our present system is geared to verbal learning, and if your children are not verbal learners, they don't fit the system. Most testing methods are limited to a linear, sequential format geared to verbal content. Visual or kinesthetic students often are labeled "slow learners."

One such student was Carlos. He was a handsome eight-year-old with dark brown hair, beautiful brown velvet eyes, and a shy grin. He came from a bilingual family that emphasized strong academic performance. He, however, was a dreamer, involved in his own fantasy world of adventure on submarines and trips to outer space. He spoke rarely in class, never in group discussions.

The focus of Carlos's interest was art; he drew complex spacecraft and underwater vehicles while I instructed the class about vowel blends or capitalization. During a writing or math assignment he would stare off into space for minutes at a time and then meticulously form his letters or numbers. It took him forever to write a sentence or finish a series of math problems; he rarely finished an assignment in the alloted time.

Two months after school started, I began to notice that Carlos was one of the first children to close his eyes during an imagery exercise and that he enthusiastically verbalized his images. The children and I listened raptly as he told us what he "saw" during the "Undersea Adventure" exercise:

> I walked down the tunnelway and entered the bubble room. I
> felt strange in the room. There was water all around it. But in
> the room there was no water, only soft pillows. Outside there

FIVE

39

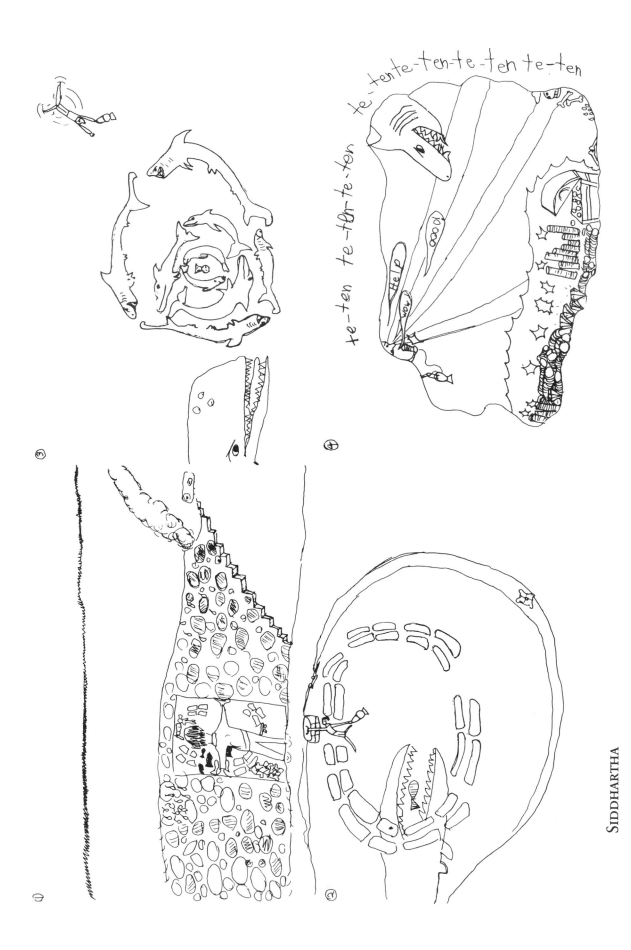

te-ten te-ten-te-ten-te-ten te-ten

te-ten te-ten-te-ten

SIDDHARTHA

was a skateboard, and I got on the skateboard and skated all the way up to the top of the room. There was a wheel of fish at the top, with a shark in the middle and killer whales and dolphins all around. Then it was time to come back here.

After hearing his responses to many imagery exercises, I noticed that every time we closed our eyes and imaged, an entire movie, with a complex plot, unfolded for Carlos. Many times he would draw pictures of his images after an exercise and then describe to us what had happened.

As we accepted his visual images, Carlos gained more and more confidence to *speak* his ideas. He became more and more articulate. As the months progressed, Carlos began to "dream" less in class and get more work done.

Carlos brings to mind another visual thinker who became a famous artist. This child was a dismal failure at school. He stubbornly refused to do anything but paint; his paintbrush became the extension of his arm. His father was an art teacher himself, so this young boy was surrounded by visual delights and the wonderful smell of oil paints. He tried to re-create his home atmosphere at school by taking the pigeons from his father's studio to class with him, but he refused to sit still to learn to read, write, and count.

The father, realizing his son's innate ability as an artist and his love for the visual, finally took him out of school at age ten and let him wander the streets of his town, enjoying the street scenes, sketching and painting as he pleased. When it was time for him to take entrance exams into an academic art school, he passed in one day tests devised to last a month. He had learned to prime his memory with visual cues.

This learner, Pablo Picasso, was fortunate to have the opportunity to experience the street life of Madrid.[1] In our current society, this educational approach is rarely possible.

WORDS LIMIT LEARNING

I think we put too much stress on our kids to read, write, and speak. Our overemphasis on the written and spoken word inhibits expression in other ways. We are a society that loves to categorize and label.

As I push my cart up and down the aisles of the local supermarket, I am amazed at the way mothers and fathers of all cultural backgrounds insist on having their young children name food products. "What's this?" the father asks. "Soup." "That's right, a can of soup. And what's this?" "Peach." "That's right, a peach."

What I don't hear is, "Hold this. Feel the shape, the weight, the texture of it. Touch it to your cheek. Smell it. Notice all the colors."

Why do we limit what our children know to the simple monosyllabic label that represents an object that has a scent, texture, shape, taste, and is a visual delight? What about the sound of a peach? It may evoke a lullaby.

Some children receive so much attention for being "cute" verbally that they don't know how to turn it off. They believe that if they're not talking incessantly, they might not be loved or recognized.

Hillary was such a child. She had highly developed verbal skills and verbal memory. She delighted in relating stories about her trips to Jerusalem and Europe, and her fact retention about the lives and customs of people in these countries was amazing. Petite and enthusiastic, she had received much attention from adults over the years for being an articulate, precocious, pretty child.

However, at times she was a bit haughty. She had difficulty with friendships because she was extremely opinionated about everything. "You're supposed to do it this way, Jill." "You pronounced that wrong, Maureen." "You're not very good at drawing, are you, Max?" As the litany continued, it was no surprise that some of the children lost their patience with her and began to tell her to shut up!

One day, while listening to Hillary express her ideas after an imagery exercise, I noticed how much she *moved* while talking. Her hands and arms gestured, her head tilted, her eyes brightened. Her face came alive with expression. Her whole body was engaged in describing her image. She looked as if she were acting out a ballet of her ideas.

It occurred to me, while watching her move, that she might be a kinesthetic learner who had had little chance to express that side of herself. I asked if she'd rather dance her images than tell us about them. After some initial reluctance, she got up and began to sway back and forth, miming strands of a willow tree gently dancing in a soft summer breeze. She slowly lifted her arms, took one final look at me for reassurance, and moved gently around the room like the soft breeze she had become. These movements expressed so much more about her than all of her words combined.

We were all quite surprised and captivated. Hillary was ecstatic! She had found another way to express herself—a way that had been denied to her by the limitation of her constant chatter.

There are risks when trying a new form of expression, but the benefits outweigh the risks. One new form of expression unlocks another. After *moving* her images, Hillary felt more confident to try art and poetry.

During a poetry exercise the following week, I suggested that she "move" her ideas before attempting to put them on paper. She walked around the classroom, stopped, sat down on the floor, and moved her arms as if re-arranging something. She then wrote:

> When you lie on the ground
> Looking at the clouds
> You also watch the wind blow them
> Around and around

If a child can draw an image, hum it, or move through it first, he or she may then be able to talk or write about it more easily. Try it with your own child. You'll be delighted with the results.

EXERCISE 6

An Undersea Adventure

AGE: 5 through adult
EXERCISE: 5 minutes
FOLLOW-UP: 15 minutes

Close your eyes and focus your attention on your breath. (*Pause*) Now imagine that you are walking down to the beach. It is a beautiful, sunny day, and you enjoy the sound of the surf. (*Pause*) As you walk along the beach you notice a trap door in the sand. You lift up the trap door, and there is a stone stairway leading down under the sand. You walk down the stairway, feeling perfectly safe, and find yourself in a long tunnelway. You walk through the tunnelway until you come to a room at the end of the tunnel. You enter the room, which looks like a glass bubble. You realize that you are in a glass room under the sea. Beautiful colored fish are swimming outside. You notice that there is a submarine and a diving suit in the room for your use if you choose to venture out into the sea. There is also a pillowed chair in the middle of the room if you wish to sit down. You now have a minute of clock time equal to all the time you need to enjoy all the wonders of the sea.

(*After a minute*) Now it is time to return. (*Pause*) You walk back through the tunnelway, up the stairs toward the sunlight. You close the trap door, knowing that you can return here whenever you wish. You leave the beach and become aware of sitting here, fully present.

I am going to count to ten. Join me at the count of six, opening your eyes at ten, feeling fully alert and with full recollection of your adventure. One . . . two . . . three . . . four . . . five . . . six . . . seven . . . eight . . . nine . . . ten.

Explain to your children that in Exercise 7 they will explore a place in time and space that they have never visited before. They may go either backward or forward in time and act as journalists who have come to learn as much as possible about this undiscovered place. When they return from their explorations, they will write a report about what they have observed. Ask them to pay attention to all of the colors, sounds, smells, tastes, and feelings they have on this trip.

ADAM

EXERCISE 7
Time Traveling

AGE: 8 through adult
EXERCISE: 5–10 minutes
FOLLOW-UP: 15 minutes

Close your eyes and find a comfortable position in your chair that you can maintain for several minutes. Follow your breath in and out of your nostrils. As you follow your breath you will notice that you are becoming very relaxed, yet alert. Now let go of any thoughts or expectations that you may have, and allow your imagination to float free.

Imagine now that you walk outside this room and there is a time machine in front of you. Walk around the time machine, noticing its shape and controls. You climb into the machine and set the controls for a time in history either many years past or many years in the future. When you set the controls to visit the time in history that you choose, you feel yourself being gently yet swiftly lifted and transported to the time you have chosen. As you move, light seems to move around you. When you land, you begin to explore this new land. You notice the environment, the life forms. If there are any creatures in this world, try to communicate with them and find out about their culture, their family life, what they eat, and how they live. If they have music, you will be able to bring back a song from their world. Notice their art. You may wish to find a particular person or creature and to spend some time with this being. Now you have several minutes of clock time to carry out your explorations in the world you are in now, and this is all of the time you will need, because you can experience days or weeks or months or even years of experience before it is time to leave here.

(*After 2–3 minutes*) It is now time for you to leave this world and to climb back into the time machine. You may wish to tell the creatures you have befriended that you will return another time. Set the dials in the time machine to the present, and return safely here to this room. When you open your eyes you will remember everything you saw and felt in detail, and you will be able to write a full report on your travels.

Join me at the count of six as I count to ten, and when you open your eyes you will be alert and have full recollection. One . . . two . . . three . . . four . . . five . . . six . . . seven . . . eight . . . nine . . . ten.

This exercise can be repeated once a month so that children may have the opportunity to learn more about the life systems of the worlds they visited. It provides rich material for discussing family structures, transportation systems, food, environment, music, and communication. This exercise, although particularly applicable to high school students, can be used with younger children as well.

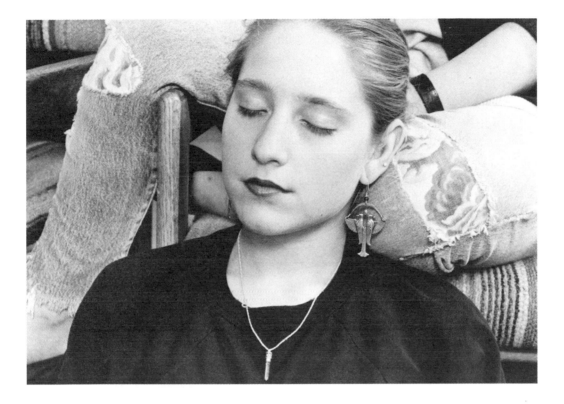

RESPONSES TO "TIME TRAVELING"

MY TRIP BACK IN TIME

I was in my backyard playing on the swing. Then I heard a big crash so I jumped off my swing and went to look. When I got there I saw a round ball. I looked all around for a door. I couldn't find one, but then after I walked around about a hundred times I found the door.

I opened it and inside there was a bright orange seat. In front of it there was a computer with buttons all around it. On one of the buttons it said "backward" and on the other it said "forward." But there were other buttons too. Another one said "go" and another one said "stop."

I decided that I would take a trip with the little round ball. Then I found out what backward and forward meant. Backward meant back in time and forward meant forward in time.

I got myself something to eat. Then I got in the ball spaceship and I pressed "go." Right after I pressed "go" it started to move. It went very fast. I looked out the window and I saw the clouds. I was way up in the sky.

Then I landed in a place back in time. I saw ladies with pretty dresses. The men had black suits on and tall hats. I looked all around. It was a pretty place. I saw old fashioned schools. The children were writing the best because they didn't want to be hit by a ruler. Everyone was rushing back and forth. Then I saw a little girl. She just told me a little about the place.

Then I had to go back so I said bye to all the people. I got into the ball space ship. Then I pressed "go" and flew off with the spaceship. Then in a couple of seconds I was back in St. Augustine in the class. I liked that trip a lot.

—*Laura, age eight*

TIME MACHINE

My journey was into the future. My time machine was big and shaped like an egg. It was white and light blue. On my journey I saw many things, like all the people were nude. They did not drive cars but they flew around in the city with some kind of rocket on their back. The air was so polluted that you could see all the dead fish and plants on the shore. The rivers and lakes were polluted with trash and chemicals from careless campers and companies. All the dolphins and whales were beached along the shore. The birds that used to swim in the ocean no longer could because there were oil spills and the oil got on their feathers and made it hard for them to fly. Many fish and other organisms died from lack of oxygen. I took myself up above the pollution to where there were no buildings, nothing around me. Just cool, cool air.—*Alicia, age sixteen*

NOTE TO PARENTS AND TEACHERS

Exercise 8 can be used in conjunction with a lesson in geography or social studies to help your child or students imagine the life of other cultures and countries (e.g., Latin America, ancient Egypt, Africa). Parents find this exercise helpful when preparing for a trip abroad. It is fun for children to imagine what a country and the people will be like and then to visit and check out the accuracy of their imagination.

EXERCISE 8
Cultural Anthropology

AGE: 8 through adult
EXERCISE: 5–10 minutes
FOLLOW-UP: 15 minutes

Close your eyes and begin to focus your attention on your breath. Give yourself the suggestion that with each exhalation your body becomes more and more relaxed. (*Pause*) Imagine that your body is becoming circular, that you are taking the form of a ball, a sphere, or a globe. You will notice next that this sphere is moving and in fact that you now are hurtling at very great speed across vast reaches of space, traveling on and on until you find yourself gradually slowing down and coming to a stop. Your body is resuming its normal shape, and you look around to discover where you have arrived. It is a strange land, a new world that you are in, and it is very interesting for you to explore.

Investigate this world, its life forms, its environment. If there are people in this land, communicate with them and find out all you can about their culture, family life, what they eat, and how they live. If they have music, you will be able to bring back a song from their world. Notice their art. You now have several minutes of clock time equal to all of the time that you need to carry out your explorations of this land. This is all of the time that you will need because you can experience days or weeks or months or even years before it is time to leave this land. Begin. (*Pause 3 minutes*)

Now it is time to come back. You take one last look around, noticing the colors, shapes, sounds, smells, and tastes. You then find yourself moving quickly again through time and space in the form of a ball and gently land here with your body resuming its normal shape. (*Pause*)

In a moment I will count to ten. Join me at the count of six, opening your eyes at ten, feeling relaxed and alert and ready to draw or write about your visit to another culture. One . . . two . . . three . . . four . . . five . . . six . . . seven . . . eight . . . nine . . . ten.

RESPONSE TO "CULTURAL ANTHROPOLOGY"

DISCOVERING THE NEW WORLD

It was early in the morning and I was trying to convince the king and queen that the world was round. As I told them this they got to thinking that I was insane so they called their guards and had me thrown out.

I got so mad that I decided to prove it, but first I would have to find a crew and buy a few ships. But that wasn't my only problem; the big problem was that I had no money. So I began scouting around for a job. After a few days I finally got a job at a bar. It didn't pay very much but it was something.

Two years went by and I had enough money to buy five ships. Now all I had to do was find myself a crew. Luckily I had a friend named Jack to help and in a month we set sail. It took us 6 months before we hit land. We came ashore and there were people there. Not knowing how they were called, I called them Indians. They took me to their camp and gave me some dried meat which I didn't like. We stayed there three months and then we had to go back. We told the king about the new land and he didn't believe us so we kept it to ourselves.

—*Bobby, age twelve*

Improving Skills through Imagery

@ @ @ @ @ @ @

Have you ever noticed how eager young children are to learn about everything? And how they are constantly moving while doing so? Whether they are painting at the easel, stirring cake batter, or building blocks, their whole body is involved. And learning occurs during this movement.

As children get older, they use their bodies less and less while involved in learning. Most of the school day consists of sitting, listening, and writing. Just think of how much brain power they are wasting by not moving their bodies. This mental potential can be recovered through the use of imagery.

Our physical body responds to imagery. As we "image" a particular movement, our brain transmits this knowledge to the muscles in our body. Athletes use this technique to consciously improve skills. Arnold Schwarzenegger, a five-time Mr. Universe and a four-time Mr. Olympia, reports that weight lifting is an exercise in "mind over matter." "As long as the mind can envision the fact that you can do something, you can. I visualize myself being there already having achieved the goal. Working out is merely the physical follow through; a reminder of the vision you're focusing on." [1]

Children use this form of mental rehearsal in athletics without even thinking about it. I have asked thousands of children how they get ready in their minds for a sports event. These are some of their responses.

> Oh, I see myself at the foul line and feel the texture of the basketball in my hands. I then feel my body braced for the shot and I see the ball going into the net after I release it from my fingertips.

> I often spend time in bed at night before a meet and imagine myself going through my whole gymnastics routine. That way I get to see where I might make mistakes and how I can improve.

> I practically feel myself stroking through the water before I swim. I always daydream about it before a race. And I always know that I'm going to win.

Todd

When I ask them if these mental images help, the answer is always yes. If I ask them whether anyone has ever taught them how to use this mental imagery, the answer is always no. "Oh, no, I don't tell anybody about it; they'd think I was crazy."

These children use mental rehearsal naturally, while professional coaches now have to *teach* their athletes the skills of visualization and imagery. Professor Richard Suinn, head of the Department of Psychology at Colorado State University, "has Olympic skiers practice imagining their ski runs and mentally correcting errors they have made in physical practice."[2]

After discussing the improvement of sports performance with imagery, my next question to students is how they could use this type of mental practice to improve their schoolwork. Here are some of their answers:

> Oh, I guess I could imagine myself improving my math or doing well on a test.

> I could write my spelling words in my mind while trying to memorize them. I could see myself getting all A's.

I once tutored an eight-year-old girl, Elise, who had very poor visual perceptual skills. She was not an aural/visual learner and could not remember the spelling of a word when she saw and heard it. I used kinesthetic (body) imagery to help Elise remember. In working with the vocabulary word *sketch,* I asked her first to look at the written word; she then wrote it in large letters in the air with her hand while correctly saying the letters and the word itself. Next she closed her eyes and imagined writing the word perfectly in the air. Then she repeated both the actual writing of the word in the air and the mental imagery of the same.

I then asked her to imagine sketching her favorite picture. She did so and then wrote the word *sketch* correctly on her paper. Elise remembered the spelling and meaning of the word because that memory was now located in her brain *and* her body. And through repeated practice, the memory remained.

We can use mental imagery to improve all skills: athletic, academic, and artistic. Children are improving their musical skills by using mental rehearsal to practice an instrument, whether it is piano, saxophone, or voice. Children can see, feel, and hear themselves play an entire musical composition in a minute or two of eyes-closed imagery time and then go on actually to play the piece perfectly. A piano teacher tells me how she uses short relaxation and visualization techniques to help her students "hear" a piece before they play it with the correct phrasing and tempo. She then has them mentally practice so that they can feel their fingers moving fluidly across the keys. Afterward, they play with deeper feeling, skill, and appreciation for their art form.

Jean Houston and Robert Masters of the Foundation for Mind Research have developed numerous "psychophysical" exercises to help people use more of their body/mind abilities. In an exercise known as multitracking, Dr. Houston suggests moving as many parts of your mind and body at once to exercise all of the connections in the brain. The next exercise is an adaptation of that suggestion for children.

Rub Your Belly, Tap Your Head

AGE: 3 through adult
TIME: 3 minutes

This exercise is fun and invigorating, and clears the cobwebs from tired minds and bodies. Children are always surprised at how many things they can do at once. One nine-year-old boy told me, "I discovered I can do more than one thing at a time; I always thought all I could do was run and scream at the same time!"

Start by standing with your weight evenly balanced over both feet. Now take a deep breath and relax. Begin by rubbing your belly with your right hand, feeling both your hand and your belly. Now tap your head with your left hand . . . very gently up and down. Start to tap your right foot . . . and imagine that in the left side of your brain you are licking a chocolate ice-cream cone. On the right side a monkey is riding a bicycle. Now begin to sing, "We all live in a yellow submarine. . . ." Continue for about one minute.

You may extend Exercise 10 by having your child or class think of a skill they wish to improve, such as throwing a pass, roller-skating, or typing. Now suggest to them that they practice this skill physically in the spot in which they are standing. Stop. Now suggest to them that they practice this skill with the imaginary or kinesthetic body. They should actually see and feel themselves practicing this skill perfectly without actually moving. Now suggest that they practice again physically. Stop. And again with the imaginary body. Stop. Once again perform the skill physically. Stop, and notice whether there was any improvement.

After doing this exercise, many children report seeing an approach to performing a particular skill that they have never tried before. They may notice mistakes they are making, or they may learn that they perform better when relaxed. Confidence in our abilities grows as we can imagine performing perfectly. The brain and the central nervous system don't know the difference between a deeply engraved image and an actual event. If we can deeply imprint an image, it is just as strong as actually doing the action.

Kinesthetic body exercises can be done with eyes open or shut. I find it more effective to close my eyes—it shuts out distractions.

EXERCISE 10

Use Your Imaginary Body

AGE: 5 through adult
TIME: 3–5 minutes

The purpose of this exercise is to show children how quickly and efficiently they can increase physical skills through mental rehearsal. In this exercise they'll rotate their body around to the right without moving their feet, to see how far they can rotate before and after mental rehearsal.[3]

Stand balanced on both feet and breathe gently. Raise your right hand to eye level and focus your attention on your thumb. With your feet still, move your arm around to the right, looking at your thumb, and see how far around you can go. Don't strain yourself. Now mark an imaginary spot on the wall where you have turned, and bring your arm back to starting position.

Now we're going to repeat this exercise without moving our arms, using only our eyes. Without lifting your arm, move your head around again to the right, leading with your eyes, and mark an imaginary spot on the wall. This spot will probably be farther than the first one you marked with your thumb. Now come back to center. Relax and breathe deeply.

We will now do this exercise with our kinesthetic body. The kinesthetic body is our imagined muscular sense, or imaginary body. Luke Skywalker, in *The Empire Strikes Back,* learned how to use the skills of the kinesthetic body in learning how to use the Force. Any skill you practice with your kinesthetic body is learned by your physical body. You may even feel your muscles moving as you do this exercise, but you won't be consciously moving your physical body.

Now close your eyes and lift your kinesthetic right arm. This is not your physical right arm, but your imaginary right arm. Now get a sense of your imaginary right thumb, and begin to move your imaginary right arm around to the right as far as you can go. You go past the first spot you marked and past the second, and you mark a spot on the wall with your imaginary right thumb as far as you can go. Now slowly bring your imaginary body back to starting position and lower your imaginary arm. Open your eyes.

Now we will repeat this exercise with your physical right arm. Take a deep breath and lift your physical right arm to eye level, and rotate your

58

right arm all the way around to the right. Go as far as you can go without straining. Mark a spot on the wall. Now bring your arm back to starting position and notice how you feel. Did you move farther this time than you did at the beginning of this exercise? You may wish to repeat this exercise with your left arm.

There is usually at least a 30 percent improvement after practicing this exercise. Adults and children alike are amazed at the power of mental imagery to improve a skill.

EXERCISE 11

Skill Rehearsal with a Master Teacher

AGE: 7 through adult
EXERCISE: 5 minutes
FOLLOW-UP: 15 minutes

In this exercise we use the image of a "Master Teacher" to help improve a specific skill.[4] *Begin by choosing a skill that you wish to improve or perfect. It may be soccer, writing, painting, or whatever it is that you wish to improve.*

Stand with your weight evenly balanced over your feet and take a deep breath. In your mind's eye, see yourself involved in the skill you have chosen to improve. Now practice it for a minute with your physical body as well as you can in the space in which you are standing.

(*After a minute*) Now practice it for a minute with your kinesthetic body.

(*After a minute*) Now sit down in a comfortable position and close your eyes. Focus your attention on your breath, following your breath in . . . and . . . out . . . of your nostrils. As you continue to breathe, you find yourself becoming more and more relaxed.

Now imagine that you are out hiking and you find yourself on a path in a very thick forest. The forest seems very friendly, so you continue down a path until you come to a glen of very tall trees. As you approach this group of trees, you notice that one of the trees has a door in it. You open the door and walk into a small hallway. The hallway leads you down a stone staircase. You begin to go down the stairs, down . . . down . . . down. Finally you come to a great room that is filled with wonderful inventions that you have never seen before. You walk around the room amazed by all that you see. You follow another corridor until you find yourself in a room that feels very peaceful and familiar. There you meet the Master Teacher of your skill, someone who can teach you all you want to know. This Teacher may speak to you in words or in actions; either will be very effective for you. You have three minutes of clock time equal to all of the time that you need to learn from your Master Teacher.

(*After 3 minutes*) Now you will leave your Master Teacher, thanking this person and knowing that you can return any time you wish. Walk back through the corridor through the room of the marvelous inventions, up the staircase, and out through the door in the tree. You close the door and walk back through the forest. And then you find yourself sitting here. When you are ready, open your eyes, stand up, and rehearse your skill with your physical body. (*Pause 1 minute*) Stop. Rehearse your skill with your kinesthetic body. (*Pause 1 minute*) Now again with your physical body. (*Pause 1 minute*) Now this time, as you do it again with your kinesthetic body, notice if there is more for you to learn about your skill. Is there a new approach that you can try? If so, try this with your kinesthetic body and then again physically. Notice any improvement that you have made, and notice, too, how you feel about your ability.

RESPONSES TO THE "MASTER TEACHER" EXERCISE

Children have reported invoking Pélé to improve soccer kicks, Haydn to tutor piano, and Mark Twain to put some humor into their writing. They also call on the help of friends, relatives, and mythological characters. The following responses were from a group of third-graders.

> I was with Haydn again today. He told me I must practice more to get better. He said that I must look at the notes and then I would get to a new book.

> As I breathed in I felt like I was going down the steps. Then I found myself going into the sea and Neptune taught me how to swim.

> I wanted to practice running and my teacher was Bruce Jenner. He said "Keep your pace and keep running."

> I found this exercise very scary. I didn't like going down the steps. So I just waited until the exercise was over and opened my eyes.

When children say that they find an exercise scary, I ask if they want to discuss what they find fearful. The child who expressed fear about the Master Teacher exercise was afraid of the dark and was scared that he'd never get out of the tree. I explained to him that in his imagination he has many choices. He may brightly light the steps going down, he may take an ally to protect him or to guard the door to assure his safe return, or he may choose—as he did—not to go. He may also tune me out at any time he wishes and create a whole new scenario. He may decide to meet his Master Teacher on the baseball diamond!

I think that it is important, however, to reassure such children that they are safe and to give them the time and opportunity to express their fears. Don't judge them by saying, "Oh, that's silly; nothing can happen. You know it's only your imagination." The imagination has dark images as well as bright ones, and these must be respected and addressed.

Exercise 12 can be modified when teaching about the lobes of the brain by suggesting that your child or adolescent focus attention on the frontal lobe, which provides the capacity for foresight and the ability to plan for the future; the temporal lobe, which acts as the hearing center and may be where memories are permanently stored; the parietal lobe, which receives sensations of touch and spatial information; and the occipital lobe, which monitors sight. An alternative would be to focus on the left and right hemispheres and the corpus callosum, which acts as a telegraph system transmitting messages back and forth between the two hemispheres. Making the brain more accessible through imagery exercises encourages conscious awareness of the brain/mind/body connection.

EXERCISE 12

Making Friends with your Brain

AGE: 9 through adult
TIME: 5–10 minutes

Close your eyes and begin to focus your attention on your breath, giving yourself the suggestion that with each exhalation your body becomes more and more relaxed. Good. Now bring your attention up into your brain, and as you breathe in . . . and . . . out, imagine your brain pulsing in . . . and . . . out. Become aware of the shape of your brain within your skull, noticing its weight and size.

Now lift your hands and, without actually touching your head, bring them as close to your brain as possible, about a half inch from your skull. Feel the warmth between your hands and your brain. Feel the energy radiating from your brain to the palms of your hands. Feel your brain as a living, breathing organism. Begin to make friends with your brain. (*Pause*)

Now put your hands down while still focusing attention on your brain. Send your brain messages of gratitude for the wonderful job it does, and request that it continue to function with greater skill and capacity each day. Suggest to your brain that it send healing messages throughout your body for better functioning. (*Pause*)

Now, as I count to five, bring yourself back to full waking consciousness, feeling relaxed, alert, and with greater awareness of your brain. One . . . two . . . three . . . four . . . five.

SEVEN

Making Self-Expression Easy

◎ ◎ ◎ ◎ ◎ ◎ ◎

There is no limit to the creativity with which children write when inspired by their own imagination. They can move into the future, review the past, and create inventions to do their homework. If you suggest an imagery exercise in which they are to solve environmental problems or negotiate a peaceful settlement to a war, there is no end to the creative solutions you will hear. Never again will you hear, "I have nothing to write about."

Children are natural storytellers, and an imagery exercise opens the door to the expression of colorful dreams and visions. It is one way of putting daydreams to work; the child is actually given permission to daydream during a specific time period and then to put that image into words, pictures, or movement. Guided imagery is so effective in teaching writing because it allows children to put their immediate experiences into words.

Imagery also encourages the less verbal child to express his or her ideas. Sometimes children feel that they have nothing to say of value or that others say it better.

Such a student was Janine. A left-handed eight-year-old, Janine was very reluctant to articulate her ideas in class. When she spoke, her voice was so quiet that it was hard to hear her. She had great difficulty reading aloud in a group. She reversed many letters in written work as well as in reading.

After an imagery exercise in which we took a trip to an imaginary planet, she became verbally more expressive. While on that planet the children were to act as explorers, taking note of what life might be like there, how life forms communicated, how they lived, what their family or social structures might consist of. The children had two minutes of eyes-closed imagery time to make their survey.

When we finished our journey, Janine related the following:

> My sailboat took me close to this faraway land and then I had to
> take a dolphin the rest of the way. The people there were all very

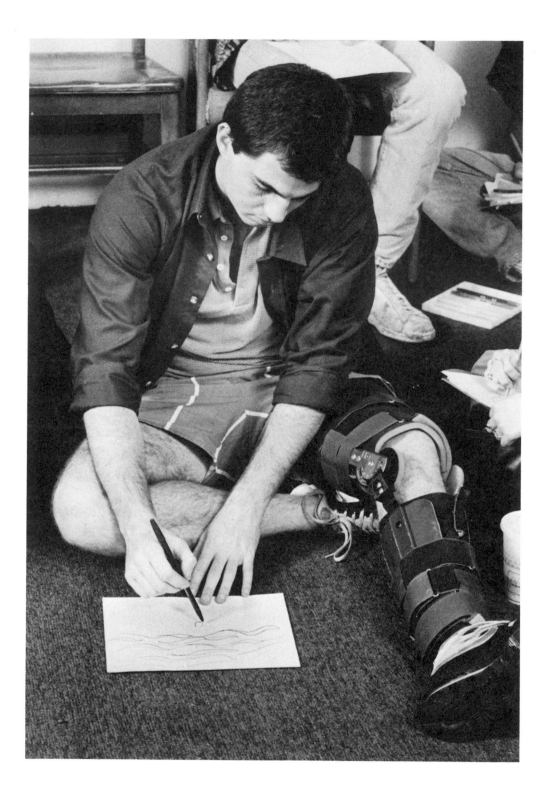

little but they had big mothers and fathers. The little people saw me coming and they made a big meal. Their foods were all different flavor jellies. They had orange halls too. Outside the orange halls you could see everything outside, but nobody could see inside. And then I got to meet the little person's mother and father. They thought I was strange because I was not big like the mother and father and I was not small like them. They put me in a special costume like the ones they wear.

A month later we repeated the same exercise. Janine again visited the land of the very little people and continued her adventures.

Today I went back to the land of the very little people. I decided to ask what the name of their planet was so I wouldn't have to call it the land of the little people. They told me they didn't really have a name and I could make one up. It took me a while to make up my mind. In the meantime, they said they would show me their spring garden. There were lots of little round things that were greenish-brownish that grew out of the ground. They had little glasses of water next to them. I said "Those aren't flowers, they're just little balls." So they dipped one of the balls in the water and they all yelled "rose." They took it out and dried it and there they had a beautiful rose. And they could do that with any kind of flower or bush. Then I sat down to figure out a name for their planet. I thought it might be nice if it was a name that made sense about them. Well, there were lots of flowers and trees, and everybody was happy. So I could mix up the words "flower" and "tree" and it would be "Free." Then it would make sense because they are all so happy and free. I decided on that and when I told them they all loved the name. Then I had to leave. It was a wonderful adventure.

Within two months Janine improved both her speaking and writing skills. As she gained confidence in the expression of her own images, she entered more freely into class discussions. Her voice volume and tone changed, and her oral reading became clear and confident. She stopped reversing letters in reading and writing.

I am not attributing these improvements solely to the use of guided imagery, but it was clear that Janine's verbal expression improved through the use of the exercises.

LANGUAGE ARTS AND READING

Children love to read their own stories and those of their classmates. They also learn to read best when reading something of personal meaning. After an imagery exercise, you may suggest to your young children or class that they draw the pictures they saw in their mind. They can then dictate their story to you, or to an older person who can write the words. The children then read their stories aloud. What pride they feel in writing and reading aloud their own stories. You can further build vocabulary skills by using the words that appear in the story to illustrate phonics and spelling rules.

After an imagery exercise, the following story was drawn and then dictated to me by Taro, a seven-year-old boy labeled a "nonreader" by his teacher. He then read his story aloud to the group, surprised by and proud of his newfound ability to read.

> When I looked into the mirrors I saw a rainbow forming and in the very middle ring of the rainbow there was a black streak and it was getting pushed down. When it got to the middle it turned into one small dot and slowly disappeared. And then I realized that it was the spot I didn't believe in myself. And when I learned that, I felt myself lifting off the ground and starting to fly like Jonathan Livingston Seagull. Then I started to learn to control my body and I could fly fast and slow and upside down. And then I felt like I was turning into a new person.

CREATIVE WRITING

After experiencing a rich visual image, a child can paint the image with words:

> *The Maple Leaf*
> by Jessica
> The color of the leaf
> is like an orange sunset
> The texture of the leaf
> is like a cobblestone road
> The smell of the leaf
> is the sweetest smell yet
> But the taste of the leaf
> is heaven.

This poem was preceded by an imagery exercise that I did with my third-grade class introducing them to the sensual pleasures of autumn leaves. On a trip to the East Coast, I collected leaves of many varieties, colors, shapes, and sizes. The children from my class had grown up in southern California and had never seen the brilliant display of fall color. Without showing them the leaves, I asked the children to close their eyes and use all of their senses as they explored what I was about to give them.

> Sit in a comfortable position and close your eyes. Put your hands, palms up, on your thighs. Focus your attention on your breath, and as you breathe, your body and mind become more and more relaxed. (*Pause*) Imagine that you are sitting under your favorite tree and a gentle breeze begins to blow. (*Pause*) You feel the leaves as they fall from the tree. (*Drop the leaves slowly over the children*) Still with your eyes closed, pick up a leaf and hold it in your hands. Feel the veins of the leaf and notice its shape and size. Imagine what color it may be. Rub the leaf on your cheek and notice its texture. Smell it. . . . What does it remind you of? Imagine what it tastes like. You may get up, if you wish, and move like the gentle descent of autumn leaves. (*Pause*) When you are ready, slowly open your eyes.

The response to this exercise illustrated to me how important the use of the senses is in learning.

> I see leaves dancing in the breeze
> Some are yellow, green and red,
> Some look like things you never saw before.
> Mine smells like oak and is surely the best.
> The texture of the leaf smells red
> The shape of the leaf reminds me of a hand,
> When I hold it up I can see the shadow of the veins.

In this poem, "the texture smells red." This child crosses a tactile sense with smell and sight. This skill, called synesthesia, is an effective tool in memory expansion. This particular student exhibited the best memory in the class and was a year ahead in math.

Of the many exercises I use to improve sensory learning, Exercise 5, "The House of Perception" (see Chapter 4), is particularly effective.

Guided imagery is an excellent tool to develop story characters from another point of view. Children relate very strongly to animals and empathize with their feelings. They reveal a great deal about themselves when they assume the role of a favorite animal. Wonderful stories emerge as the child takes on the physical characteristics and attitudes of a character they meet in the imagery exercise. These characters become multidimensional rather than flat, stereotypical cartoons.

In an imagery exercise in which the students were instructed to become their favorite animal, one child wrote the following story.

> I was walking down a stony path. I was very hot and thirsty. My mouth was watering. Suddenly I saw a pond appear so I ran over to it quickly. I ran so fast I didn't even notice I was walking on four feet. And my whiskers were tickling my cheeks. When I got to the pond I soon saw that I had changed into one of my favorite animals. A cat!! A cat that had long brown fur.
>
> I dunked my paw into the pond and licked it with the tip of my pink rough tongue. After a while I figured out that the cat I had changed into was exactly like me. I drew with my claw a picture of a cat. Even as a cat, I could draw cats better than anything.
>
> Just then I felt someone tickle my paw. "Hello," said a small voice. I looked all around but I couldn't see anyone or anything. "Look down," said the voice again. I looked down and saw a ladybug. "I'm glad someone found me," said the ladybug. "I got lost in the fog and need a home. I want to be your friend," said the ladybug. I thought, I love making friends. I always have. Being a cat doesn't have to change anything.
>
> "If I'll be your friend, will you be my friend?"
>
> "Of course," said the ladybug. "We'll have a long day tomorrow, Jenny," said the ladybug. "Since I'm a little ladybug, will you tell me a sleep story?" I did because I love to make up stories. When I woke up in the morning I didn't have whiskers. I didn't have long brown fur. I was the regular girl with red hair and freckles. I knew it was time to leave so I grabbed the ladybug and returned to the classroom.—*Jenny, age 10*

ENHANCING CULTURAL PRIDE

In 1981, I was given the opportunity to teach guided imagery in fifty culturally mixed classrooms in British Columbia, Canada. These classes included Indian and non-Indian children from kindergarten through the twelfth

grade. The Indian students were performing poorly in reading, writing, and
other verbal skills. The purpose of my work was to reinforce the natural
visual and kinesthetic learning sense of these children.

I first introduced kinesthetic imagery. I suggested to the students that
with their eyes closed they imagine themselves making a perfect foul shot in
basketball, feeling and seeing themselves move correctly. Depending upon
the age group, I suggested sports activities, such as soccer, hockey, volley-
ball, baseball, gymnastics, dancing, and jump rope. They had no difficulty
imagining themselves performing these skills.

I then introduced visual imagery, suggesting that with their eyes closed,
they imagine what it was like when they got up that morning. What was
their earliest visual memory of the day? Did they notice the sun coming in
the window? Did they see a brother or sister when they awoke? Some children reported no image at all. All they could "see" was black. I then suggested that they repeat the exercise, noticing the first sounds, smells, tastes,
or feelings they had experienced that morning. Every child had some sense
image of waking up.

My next step was to lead them in an exercise entitled "My Ancestors" in which they imagined going back in time and space to the land of their forebears, learning everything they could about life at that time. I told them that at the end of their journey they would be required to report on their findings in a drawing or a written or oral story. Penny Joy, a video consultant, video-taped their responses and replayed them for the children to see and hear themselves.

The results were impressive. Teachers consistently told us how surprised they were to witness formerly quiet students suddenly illustrating, writing, and articulating their thoughts clearly. They commented on the sense of cultural pride the Indian students exhibited in recalling their heritage. They marveled at the use of vocabulary and metaphor elicited by the imagery.[1] We were convinced that this occurred because the imagery exercise first stimulated the children's senses and took them through an experience, which they then found no difficulty in recapturing verbally.

NOTE TO PARENTS AND TEACHERS

Suggest to your children that in Exercise 13 they will learn as much as they can about their ancestors. Explain to them that their ancestors are the people related to them who lived a long time ago. They will use the feelings, thoughts, and information from this exercise to write a descriptive story about one of their ancestors or to draw a picture about how their ancestors lived. This exercise is particularly effective for children nine to twelve years old.

My Ancestors

AGE: 7 through adult
EXERCISE: 5 minutes
FOLLOW-UP: 10–15 minutes

Close your eyes and breathe deeply, following your breath in and out of your nostrils or mouth, whichever is more comfortable for you. As you continue to breathe, allow the muscles in your body to become very relaxed.

Now imagine that you are moving back in time and space very quickly to where your ancestors lived. You may even feel yourself moving, or see lights and colors flashing as you move through space and time. Notice the environment in which your ancestors live. What are they doing? They may be hunting, farming, fishing, building, cooking, singing, dancing, creating art, climbing, taking care of the young ones, or tending the animals. Whatever they are doing, watch closely so that you will be able to remember every detail about them. What do you notice about their appearance? What do you notice about their family life? What types of animals are present? What are the colors, smells, and sounds that you are aware of?

Now pick out one particular ancestor from the group. Look at him or her closely. Notice this person's age, dress, and facial expression. Now make friends with this person and ask him or her to show you around. Learn as much as you can about how your ancestors lived. You have three minutes of clock time equal to all of the time you need.

(After three minutes) Now take one last look around, noticing the colors, sounds, smells, and tastes. Say goodbye to your new friend, and come back through time and space to present time here, and become aware of your body as you sit here. I will count to ten. Join me at the count of six, opening your eyes at ten, remembering every detail about your visit with your ancestors. One . . . two . . . three . . . four . . . five . . . six . . . seven . . . eight . . . nine . . . ten.

RESPONSES TO "MY ANCESTORS"

DOWN THE NASS

My name is Janice and I went to Port Hardy in my daydream. I met three Indians there, a girl, a lady and a man. They lived in a cabin made of branches and wood and they would skin the animals and eat the meat and use the skin for clothes. They all were wearing skins and they had different kinds of faces. Their hair was black, long and braided. I went hunting with them and got a moose and two bears. They were black bears. Then we went fishing and I got two big dogfish and three spring salmon. I then helped the people build houses out of branches. We made a big fire.

Then I went down to the Nass (river) and on my way there I got some seaweed on the rocks, cleaned it and ate it. When I got to the Nass I met one person and her name was Naksy. She told me that her name in English meant Little Lady. She talked to me in Indian and I learned how to speak in Indian. After a while we went to an Indian dance and I heard drums beating and some people singing a very loud Indian song. Then later on we ate some fish and some bear meat and some seaweed. Then we all did the dance and sang and went home. Nasky lived in a long house. In the morning we went down to the beach and got some clam shells and we made jewels out of the shells.

—Janice, age eleven

OUR ANCESTORS

I was a Raven and I was flying over the tree tops and I saw some wolves and they were going to attack my people. I was a leader and I had to protect my people so I dove down at them and I got one of them in the head and I tore off his ears. While I went after him one of the wolves jumped at me and got me in the leg. I then flew up and checked my leg and it wasn't too bad so I called some other Ravens and when they were all there we dove at the wolves and they were no match for us.

We backed them up and fought them until they got off our land and told them if they ever came on our land again they would get it worse. They all left and we went back to our village and we were rewarded by the chief and the wolves never bothered us again.

Two years later the chief died and before he died he wanted

75

me to be chief because I saved our village. He was like me years ago and that was why he wanted me to be chief. The people crowned me and we buried the chief and ever since he died I have been helping the village with food and fights.

—*Steven, age thirteen*

LIVINGSTONE

EXERCISE 14

My Spaceship

AGE: 5–12
EXERCISE: 5 minutes
FOLLOW-UP: 15 minutes

*In this exercise you will act as a reporter, bringing back as much informa-
tion as you can about the planet you choose to explore. Make sure that you
use all of your senses to learn about this planet or star, using your sight,
hearing, smell, and touch, and notice what the creatures eat if there are any
creatures living there. You may wish to taste their food. Notice how they
move, how they live, what games they play, and what their families are like.*

Close your eyes and put your attention on your breath. Breathe in . . . and
. . . out gently and quietly, and imagine that you are going outside this room
to the front yard, and there you find your own spaceship that you have designed and built. You climb up into the spaceship and get ready for takeoff.
(*Pause*)

Ten . . . nine . . . eight . . . seven . . . six . . . five . . . four . . . three . . .
two . . . one . . . blast off! You gently take off above the clouds . . . up above
the Earth's atmosphere, way out into space. And as you look back toward
Earth, you see it as a ball or sphere that is moving away from you. You
look outside your spaceship window and you see far out into space. You
choose a planet or star to investigate and head your spaceship toward it.
When you land your spaceship, you decide to investigate this planet or star
and to learn as much as you can about how the creatures live, if there are
any there. You may wish to make friends with one of the creatures and have
your new friend show you around. Notice how they communicate, how
they live, and what their planet or star looks like. Notice the smells, sounds,
and tastes and how you move on this planet. (*Pause*)

Now I am going to give you two minutes of clock time equal to as much
time as you need to explore this planet. When you hear my voice again, I
will be calling you back to return to Earth. (*Pause 2 minutes*)

Now say goodbye to your new friend, climb into your spaceship, and
head back to Earth. (*Pause*) As you come closer to Earth, it starts to look
larger and larger to you. You come back into the Earth's atmosphere . . .
back through the clouds . . . and as you come closer to Earth it is easy for
you to identify your home and your school. (*Pause*)

Now you land your spaceship . . . come back into this room . . . and become aware of sitting here. In a moment I will count to five. When you are ready, open your eyes, remembering in full detail everything about your experience. You will have time to draw or write about your journey. One . . . two . . . three . . . four . . . five.

RESPONSE TO "MY SPACESHIP"

The empty space
The last horizon calls,
In a void where sound is not,
The stars shining with brilliancy
The rays of the sun seemingly
Reaching out,
Giving the eternal life and light.
Nine bodies orbiting a radiating orb,
And in turn, others orbiting these,
Until the end of time.

The Universe, the galaxy,
A void of tranquility
The unexplained vastness
Of high feasibility.
The stars and the planets
Symbols of light
Giving us power,
And hope
Through the day and the night.

—*David, age twelve*

Adventure with the Flower Fairy

AGE: 3–12
EXERCISE: 5 minutes
FOLLOW-UP: 5–15 minutes

Sometimes you can create a guided imagery exercise based on a story that a child has written. After reading my daughter Heather's story, which follows this exercise, I used her theme to create this exercise about the flower fairies. This imagery allows children to fully indulge their sense of magic and adventure.

Close your eyes and focus your attention on your breath. Gently breathe in . . . and . . . out. As you breathe quietly and calmly, your body becomes more and more relaxed. Now imagine that you are sitting outside in the grass and it's a beautiful, warm, sunny day. You are enjoying looking at all of the new spring flowers. You enjoy their colors and smells. All of a sudden you see a little person in front of you, climbing up the stem of a lovely white daisy. This person is no bigger than your middle finger and turns to you and motions to you to follow. You realize that you yourself have become little, and you hurry to follow your new friend. You now have three minutes of clock time equal to all of the time you need to have an adventure with this flower fairy.

(*After 3 minutes*) Now it is time to say goodbye to your friend and to come back here, filled with the memories of your adventure. I will count to ten. Please join me at the count of six and open your eyes, feeling alert and refreshed at the count of ten. One . . . two . . . three . . . four . . . five . . . six . . . seven . . . eight . . . nine . . . ten.

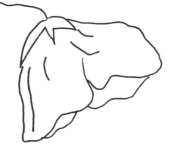

THE FLOWER FAIRIES

In a little place in Ireland there lived a girl named Mindy. She lived in a nice little cottage. Outside the cottage was every kind of flower you could think of and along side of the flowers were brick paths. The flowers were growing all around the cottage in a six foot wide row. After the paths and after the flowers, there was a big field of grass that Mindy loved to play on. Mindy was ten and had long blond hair. She lived with her mom and dad and her baby sister, Holly.

One day Mindy was sitting on the grass looking at all the flowers, when she noticed a little person about one inch tall with little wings. She was sitting on a pretty white flower talking to a ladybug. She said "No one will play with me, ladybug. Everyone is too busy." Mindy scared the ladybug and the girl by saying, "I'll play with you, what are you anyway?" The girl said, "My name is Emily. I'm a flower fairy." The rest of the day Mindy played with Emily and then Mindy was called in for dinner. After dinner she read to Holly and then went to sleep.

In the middle of the night a stream of light shined in her eye. When she woke up she found herself on a little bed with rose petals for a blanket. Mindy looked at herself and she had wings. She got up and looked around. She was in a little place that had a staircase going up to a door. She went up and knocked on the door. Emily opened it. "Good morning," she said. Mindy asked, "Why am I so little like you?" Emily said, "No time for explaining. I want you to meet the king and the queen flower fairies." They got outside and they were in the village with all these mushroom houses and mushroom shops. That's what Mindy woke up in, a mushroom house. Mindy had never seen this when she was playing because it was so well hidden under the flowers.

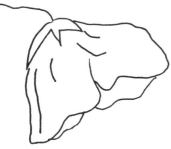

They set out for the mushroom palace. At first they walked but then Mindy figured out how to fly so they flew till they came to the great big mushroom. When Mindy saw how small Emily was compared to the king and queen, she was amazed, they were about four inches and Emily was only one. But then again Emily was not as old as the king and queen. The king and queen were very happy to have Mindy as a flower fairy. They didn't stay very long because Emily was eager to show her new friend around. When they got back to the village Emily introduced Mindy to her dad whose name was Tom, her sister, Elizabeth, and her mom, Maureen. They all live with Emily but they weren't there in the morning.

Emily and Mindy played with each other day after day and they had a lot of fun till one day Mindy heard her mom crying because she thought Mindy had run away. The next couple of days Mindy felt homesick, and she wanted to go home but none of the fairies knew how to change her back to human size. One day Emily set out real early in the morning to find out how to get Mindy to her regular size. On the way she ran into her friend the grasshopper. "Grasshopper, how can I get my friend back to human size?" "I told you, Emily, you can get any wish you want if you tell it to the white blindweed flower." "Thanks a lot, grasshopper, bye," said Emily. She ran all the way home to tell Mindy.

When Mindy heard this she said goodbye to everybody and went to the white blindweed flower. She whispered, "I would like to grow back to normal size, if you would let me, my beautiful flower." Soon Mindy found herself back in her comfortable bed. Only she and the flower fairies will remember Mindy's wonderful trip to the fairy land.—*Heather, age nine*

EIGHT

A Positive Self-Image

◎　◎　◎　◎　◎　◎　◎

One of the most important side effects of guided imagery is the development of a positive self-image. Children learn best when they think they can do it. This positive attitude carries over to everything they do. Most children look to others to reassure them of their abilities. Children who have developed a self-image as a creative and capable person don't need constant acknowledgment from others. They *know* they can do it!

The child who visualizes himself improving a particular skill, doing well on a test, or learning a new subject easily begins to believe that this is indeed possible. As the desired skill is improved or the desired test score is achieved, the child's confidence in himself is strengthened. He learns to trust in himself, in his ability to learn, in his ability to be happy.

An important fact to remember is that we optimize our learning ability when we're happy. Because of the way the brain is structured, we can't separate emotions from learning. The neural pathways between the neocortex (the cognitive brain) and the limbic system (the emotional brain) are always functioning, even in people who believe that their actions are solely directed by their intellect. Therefore, the first thing we have to do to prepare a child for learning is to create a happy frame of mind.

I was reminded of this as I led a guided imagery exercise on self-concept with a group of Native American seventh-graders in British Columbia. At the end of the exercise I asked the group what skills they imagined themselves improving. One young student saw himself catching more fish; another saw herself painting more skillfully; another saw himself improving in math. One girl came forward at the end of the class and in a voice just above a whisper said, "I didn't see myself improving in school or sports. I just saw myself as happy."

Her seventy-eight-year-old grandfather, an elder of the tribe and a teacher in the school, was present during the exercise and heard his granddaughter's response. At a teacher's meeting that afternoon we discussed the effects of imagery on learning. He told the group that this was the most important thing for his granddaughter to learn in her life—to be happy. We sometimes get so involved in filling our children with knowledge that we forget the basics.

COPING WITH STRESS

The belief that we learn best under pressure is not true. Anyone who has experienced "test anxiety" knows how tension and stress interferes with learning as well as with recall. A simple relaxation exercise can alleviate the agony that often accompanies a difficult task, whether it is performing, public speaking, or test taking. The child can gain control over unpleasant feelings of anxiety through breathing and muscle relaxation.

In a federally funded project conducted at Bell High School in Los Angeles, ninth-graders studying English as a second language scored significantly higher on tests for language proficiency than control groups.[1] This resulted from the use of relaxation and imagery exercises. Children of elementary school age from Main Street School in Los Angeles scored significantly higher on standardized tests than control groups in a three-year period.[2] This was also a result of relaxation and imagery exercises. As they visualized themselves as relaxed, successful students, they learned more quickly and retained more information.

In the classroom or at home, you may find the use of a short relaxation exercise particularly effective prior to a problem-solving session involving interpersonal relations. The children, as well as the adults, become relaxed enough to talk about hurt feelings in a productive manner. They learn to identify their own negative feelings and to talk about how the negative behavior of others affects them. And solutions become much more creative.

The following exchange occurred between two kindergarten students. These girls were part of a triangle whose members were constantly manipulating each other. We did a short relaxation exercise before discussing the current problem. You may agree with me that this level of exchange is unusually mature for five-year-olds.

> *Julianna:* Anya, you really hurt my feelings when you didn't let me play outside with you and Jennifer and Michelle.
>
> *Anya:* I didn't mean to hurt your feelings but I just didn't want to play with you then.
>
> *Julianna:* But you said that I could play with you when we went outside and that really made me feel left out.
>
> *Anya:* I forgot. You can play with us at lunch.[3]

FINDING AN ALLY

Children love having a personal confidant, someone to whom they can tell their joys and sorrows, someone who will champion their cause, someone who will give them advice when the future looks bleak. This confidant may take the form of a grandparent, a peer, a pet, or a stuffed animal. Or the child might create an imaginal friend. This imaginal friend often takes different forms: an owl, a beloved tree, a religious or mythic figure. Children build a very special relationship with this inner ally through the repeated use of imagery. The inner ally gains their trust and shows them different aspects of themselves.

I have worked with the Ally exercise with people of all ages, from five through seventy. The ally sometimes changes forms during the exercise. One twelve-year-old boy talked of how his ally started out to be a large granite boulder at the side of the stream. While he sat next to the boulder, a large stegosaurus stepped out of it. This prehistoric figure gave him a sense of strength. The shape-shifting showed him that one changes forms and goals throughout one's life.

In addition to using this exercise in the classroom, I used the Ally exercise as part of a workshop for children entitled "The Hero's Journey." In the workshop, the children are encouraged to learn to make full use of their physical, mental, and spiritual abilities as tools for daily living. They learn to identify ally qualities within themselves, such as courage and curiosity, and to recognize friends, family, and even enemies as allies. They learn that their sports abilities, artistic talents, and academic achievements can be considered allies. They discover that shortcomings can be considered allies as they learn from them and move beyond them.

SELF-ACCEPTANCE

Another method to help a child understand a fuller sense of self is to identify his or her fears, skills, dreams, and wishes. It is very important to help children become aware of their special gifts, talents, and abilities and to enable them to express their fears and fantasies. Possibly one of the most important things parents and teachers can do is to help children learn self-acceptance. If a child learns to fully accept herself with her strengths and frailties, she won't be so perplexed about who she is. In learning to accept herself, she will find it easier to accept others.

A power shield or crest is an excellent method to help children identify their unique abilities and qualities—their personal power and its significance. Power signifies much more than force or physical strength. Power can be used to create or to destroy. It is important to understand the gentle rhythms and balance of one's own power.

Peoples of many different cultures have used shields to display aspects of their families or tribes. On these shields are emblazoned symbols of particular skills, geographical locations, animal totems, and family or personal names.

The power shield is similar. On it the children draw symbols or pictures that represent their skills, fears, dreams, and wishes. They may choose skills they are proud of or a particular skill that needs improvement. The fears may represent a particular obstacle they are currently facing or a recurring fear that appears in dreams. Children find great relief in the symbolic rendering of recurring dreams. Dreams often reveal fantasies about the future as well. Wishes cover a broad spectrum, from material wishes, such as for a bicycle or skates, to creative intentions, such as a wish to swim with skill and endurance. This shield is a powerful representation of how a child sees himself or herself.

The Ally Within

AGE: *5 through adult*
EXERCISE: *5–10 minutes*
FOLLOW-UP: *15 minutes*

Close your eyes and focus your attention on your breath moving in . . . and . . . out . . . of your nostrils. As you continue to breathe at your own rate, imagine that you are on a path in a very thick forest. All around you are beautiful green trees, and you walk down this path toward the sound of water. You come upon a small stream, and you walk over to the stream and look at your reflection in the water. (*Pause*)

Soon you feel another presence standing next to you, and you feel completely safe. You see another reflection join yours in the water. This other presence may be that of an old, wise being, an animal, or an imaginary being who you feel is your ally, someone whom you have known for a long time, someone whom you can trust. Your ally beckons to you to follow across a small bridge that crosses the stream. You follow and find yourself climbing a hill that leads to a cave. Your ally enters the cave, sits down, and gestures for you to follow. You enter the cave and sit down, and your ally begins to tell you about yourself. (*Pause 1 minute*)

You may have a particular question you wish to ask your ally, and you do that now. You listen closely to the answer. (*Pause 1 minute*)

Your ally tells you that you may return at any time you wish. He or she will always be there waiting for you to help you with anything that you need. You thank your ally, walk back down the path over the bridge, looking once again at your reflection in the water. You notice how you feel as you walk up the path, out of the forest, and become aware of sitting here, fully present. Count to three to yourself and slowly open your eyes.

RESPONSE TO "THE ALLY WITHIN"

My Indian has come back to me on and off for several years. Mainly he has been around since I moved to Los Angeles. He never speaks to me actually verbally, but I can hear his thoughts. He suggests things and tells me what he thinks I should do when I am lost or confused. My mother introduced me to the idea of him. Sometimes I don't physically interact with him in my mind. Sometimes we just sit together and smoke a pipe. Usually I just see him doing various things and he thinks to me. Sometimes I don't even visualize him or think about him, but he helps me rationalize and interpret my feelings and actions. He's very simple and he is always by a teepee. He wears moccasins and deerskin pants and a shirt. He has long black braids and a band around his head made of leather with beads. He wears beads, a simple strand of brown, white, blue and black around his neck. His moccasins are beaded. He always looks peaceful.

—*Bekki, age sixteen*

JILL

For the next exercise, after explaining what a power shield is, provide plenty of art materials for each child to create a shield. Suggest a circular or crest shape for the shield, or be open to a more creative solution from the child. If you use a circle, I suggest sturdy paper with a twelve-inch-diameter circle predrawn on it. Cut out the circle or crest for the younger child. Use markers, watercolors, pastels, ribbons, yarn, sparkles, and whatever found objects are important to the child. This exercise and art activity are popular with ages eight through sixteen. Provide plenty of time for this activity.

Power Shield

AGE: 8–17
EXERCISE: 5–10 minutes
FOLLOW-UP: 15–30 minutes

Close your eyes and sit in a comfortable position. Breathe in slowly through your nose . . . hold it . . . and exhale. (*Repeat 3 times*) Now continue to breathe at your own rate and focus on a point in the middle of your forehead between your closed eyes. Imagine a circle in this spot that slowly begins to expand with each breath that you take. As you continue to breathe, your circle begins to grow and grow, getting larger and larger, until you and the circle are one.

Now you begin to see, sense, or imagine your dreams. Symbols may occur to you that represent past dreams, or you may imagine daydreams of future artistic or musical skills, or the way you are with your friends, family, or nature—whatever makes you feel good about yourself. (*Pause 1 minute*)

Now you begin to see or sense your personal fears. Whether these are small fears or large ones, you are perfectly safe. These may be obstacles that you are facing in your life at the present time, and an unexpected solution may occur to you. (*Pause 1 minute*)

Now you begin to see, sense, or imagine your dreams. Symbosl may occur to you that represent past dreams, or you may imagine daydreams of future events. Again, you are perfectly safe and learning from the images that present themselves. (*Pause 1 minute*)

And lastly you become aware of images that represent your wishes. These wishes may be for something you want or something you want to be. Whatever you wish, may it be healthful to you and to the planet. (*Pause 1 minute*)

Now, in a moment I will count to ten, asking you to join me counting aloud at the count of six. Please open your eyes at the count of ten, feeling alert and refreshed and able to remember specific symbols that represent your skills, fears, dreams, and wishes. You may use these to create your personal Power Shield. One . . . two . . . three . . . four . . . five . . . six . . . seven . . . eight . . . nine . . . ten.

NOTE TO PARENTS AND TEACHERS

The purpose of Exercises 18 and 19—"Me as Robot" and "Mandala"—is to illustrate the difference between functioning on automatic pilot, like a robot or a machine, and functioning in harmony with one's self and the universe.[4] Provide plenty of paper (12 by 18 inches) and markers and crayons or watercolors to illustrate the Robot and Mandala.

Discuss the meaning of the mandala before presenting the Mandala exercise. A mandala is a circular design that has a center from which the circle expands, as life grows from a cell or a plant grows from a seed. The center is the beginning of the mandala just as it is the beginning and origin of all life. The center exists in all forms—a cell, a snow crystal, the sun, the earth, a human being. We begin our drawing of the mandala from the center. An excellent resource is *Mandala* by José and Miriam Arguëlles.

During this exercise or while the mandalas are being drawn, you may wish to play Pachelbel's Canon in D.

EXERCISE 18
Me As Robot

AGE: 8 through adult
EXERCISE: 5 minutes
FOLLOW-UP: 15–20 minutes

Close your eyes and begin to focus your attention on your breath. Take three deep breaths, releasing any tension in your body with each exhalation. (*Pause*)

Now become aware of times when you have felt like a machine or a robot—times when you have functioned automatically, at the command of others. Experience that sensation in your body. How does it feel? What are the shoulds, the have-tos, the habitual patterns in your life that interfere with your personal freedom? What makes you feel like a robot? (*Pause 1 minute*)

In a moment I will give you a large piece of paper, and you will have twenty minutes to create yourself as Robot with pencil, crayons, or markers. Now slowly open your eyes. You may wish to begin by drawing a robot-shaped outline and fill it in with pictures or words that illustrate your habits and how they inhibit your freedom.

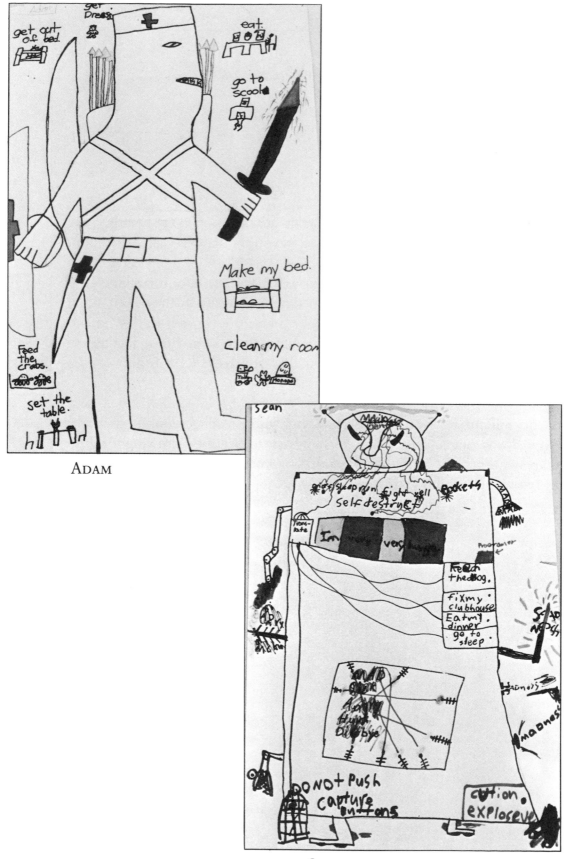

ADAM

SEAN

EXERCISE 19
Mandala

AGE: 8 through adult
EXERCISE: 5 minutes
FOLLOW-UP: 20–30 minutes

Close your eyes and begin to breathe slowly through your nostrils. Now take three deep breaths, releasing any tension that you may carry in your body as you breathe out. (*Pause*) Good. Now continue to breathe at your own rate, and focus your attention on a point in the middle of your forehead between your closed eyes. Imagine a circle in this spot that slowly begins to expand with each breath that you take. As you breathe, your circle begins to grow and grow, getting larger and larger, until you and the circle are one. (*Pause*)

Your circle continues to expand until it encompasses everyone in the room. (*Pause*) As you continue to breathe, your circle gets larger and larger and encompasses all of your friends and family and finally surrounds the entire universe. With each breath you take, you and the entire universe are one, in energy, spirit, and love. (*Pause*) Continue to breathe into your circle as you imagine yourself as Mandala, being both the center and the whole of the universe. (*Pause 1 minute*)

When you are ready, and only when you are ready, count to five to yourself and gently open your eyes, becoming aware of your physical body and of the other people around you. Take a circular piece of paper, find a spot in the room where you are comfortable, and use your markers, pastels, or crayons to create yourself as Mandala. Stay in the feeling of being one with the universe as you draw.

Children love drawing themselves as robots, and the results are quite startling. Time pressures are not the sole domain of the adult. In children's drawings, illustrations of clocks or children rushing to the bus or car pool are themes repeated often. Pictures of "getting stuck in traffic jams on the way to a friend's house," "not being ready when it is time to go," "not having enough time to do homework," and "never having time to just be" are repeated over and over.

Children illustrate the "have-tos" graphically: "When I have to feed my

dog/cat/bird/crabs/baby sister . . . get up . . . go to bed . . . set the table . . . do my wash . . . clean my room . . . be quiet . . . take out the trash . . . practice piano . . . go to school . . . brush my teeth . . . get a haircut . . . take a bath . . . clean up after my brother. . . ."

The second most repeated category is the "don'ts": "Don't get dirty . . . stay out late . . . watch TV . . . mess up your room . . . fight with your mother/sister/brother." The other habituations that are often illustrated are feelings of frustration about illness, inferior athletic skills, lack of money, lost lunches, forgotten homework, or fears about parents going away or dying. Older children and adolescents often produce illustrations that convey distress about body parts and the stress of nuclear war, gang attacks, and peer pressure to take drugs and alcohol or be sexually active. The complexities of life for today's youngster are enormous, and parents and teachers need to be aware of these.

NINE

Inner and Outer Harmony

If I know that you and I are both one, that we are not sepa-
rated and that I am not only my brother's keeper, but also
my brother, I will treat you as I treat myself—with care.
　　　　　　　　　　　　　　　　—Lawrence LeShan[1]

Occasionally, while addressing parent or teacher groups, I am asked: "Isn't
guided imagery a self-centered withdrawal? Aren't you teaching children to
hide in their fantasies, to avoid the realities of everyday life?"

The answer is no. If children and their family or class members together
learn to increase their awareness, quiet their emotions, and balance their
inner and outer lives through the consistent use of relaxation or imagery
exercises, then the result is more likely to be a *centered* self than a self-
centered individual. This centered self demonstrates qualities of respect and
love for himself or herself as well as others.

GROUP UNITY

At the end of a group imagery exercise, I am always amazed when a child
says, "I felt like I was one with everyone else in the group." These could be
the words of a five-, nine-, or fourteen-year-old; from a middle-class background, the inner city, the barrio, or the rural Northwest. They are not my
words or my subtle suggestion. They are the spontaneous words of a child
who unabashedly announces this "feeling."

When one child hears the response of another to imagery exercises, he
begins to identify his own inner experiences with that of the other. He real-
izes that his own feelings, dreams, fears, and desires are really quite similar
to those of other people. Others may express them differently, but they are
not that separate or isolated. This contributes to a feeling of group unity.

My strongest experience of the impact of guided imagery on group cohesiveness occurred with one third-grade class. I had a unique opportunity in that I had taught these same children before in kindergarten, and as we did throughout their kindergarten year, we began each day in third grade with a short centering exercise. As the school year progressed, my assistant, Donna, and I noticed a sense of group awareness unusual for third-graders.

Third-graders are notoriously cliquey. There are usually many triangles, and friendships are not easily shared. Children at this age assert their independence and individuality, and boys *never* play with girls.

What we observed in our class was quite the opposite. There were few cliques, and the boys and girls played together. It was common for fifteen children to sit together at lunch instead of the usual groups of twos and fours of other classes. I received comments from other teachers that this was the most cohesive group in the school. We also observed a very deep level of caring for one another that developed around the illness of one of the class members, Sean.

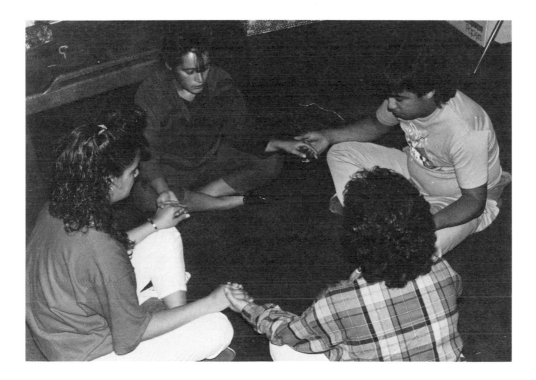

HEALING WITH LOVE

I knew Sean in kindergarten as a cheerful, sunny boy with white-blond hair, who always had a smile on his face and a song on the tip of his tongue. He did the normal amount of grumbling about his younger sister, but he seemed to have the natural ability to change a negative situation into a positive one.

During the summer between second and third grade, Sean and his family found out that he had a very serious bone tumor in his sacroiliac joint that was pressing on his sciatic nerve, causing tremendous pain. Sean came to school in September a very different child than the one I had known. He was frightened and angry about his illness, not knowing if he would recover fully and realizing that he was now different than the other children. He couldn't participate in physical activities and he was apprehensive about how the children would treat him. He felt tired much of the time and didn't feel like doing schoolwork.

In his apprehension about being different, he said that he didn't want to be singled out for special treatment, but he knew he needed our support. He told this to the class one morning during our quiet time, and all of the children began to share their feelings about his illness. They were scared too. They didn't think kids got seriously sick, and it was the first time for many of them to think about the possibility of children dying. They didn't like it that their friend was experiencing pain.

The children spontaneously suggested that during our imagery time we send love and energy to Sean. We did that while he was present, and we also did it when he went into the hospital for radiation treatments. We would image Sean in the hospital receiving our love and support. When he returned to class, he would tell us how he carried the picture of us in his mind and how it made his pain and fear go away.

It was about this time that I first heard Dr. Gerald G. Jampolsky, of the Center for Attitudinal Healing, speak of using imagery to alleviate the suffering of children who had to face life-and-death situations because of their illness or the illness of a sibling. He talked about using love to help the children let go of the fears and bad feelings they were experiencing. He also talked about how love allows us to join minds. I realized that this was exactly what the children in my class had done in sending love to Sean.

The children from the Center who accompanied Dr. Jampolsky talked about their experiences: their anger, their illness, their fear of dying, and their acceptance of death.

They wrote a book about their experiences to help other children who suffer from serious illness. This book, *There is a Rainbow behind Every Dark Cloud,* contains their stories, drawings, and the tools they found

I'm putting all my negative feelings and anger and sadness in the trash can and the balloons are taking them away.

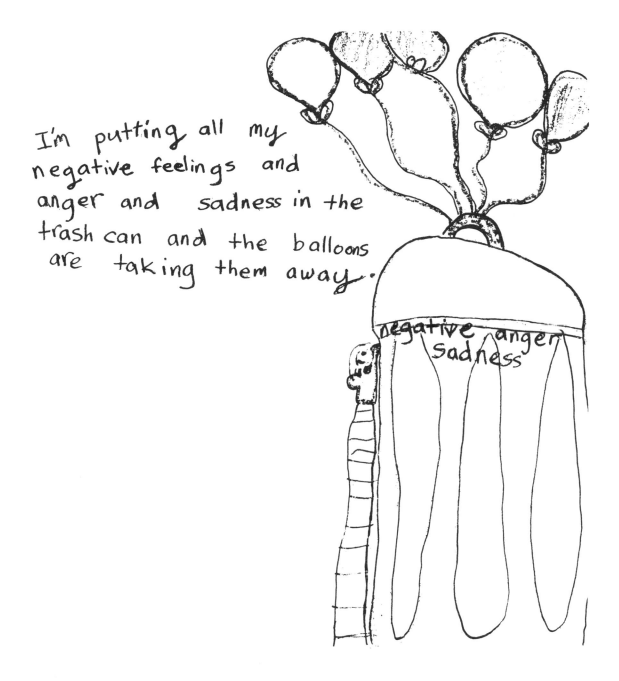

helpful in coping with their illness. One of these tools was the use of imagination exercises to deal with pain and frustration.

A ten-year-old boy with cancer from the Center led us through the following imagery exercise:

> Close your eyes and picture in your mind a large garbage can.
> Put into the garbage can any fear and anything bad that has
> happened in the past. See a large yellow balloon, filled with gas,
> being attached to your garbage can. See your garbage can go up
> into the sky and disappear.[2]

I brought this book back to Sean, and he and it became inseparable. He read and reread it and took it home to his family. He used the images in the book extensively to alleviate his pain and frustration. When he brought it back to class, everyone wanted to read it. We began to use the imagination exercise above in class, and it became a real favorite with everyone!

Some of the responses to this exercise follow:

> I threw away all the meanest things I feel and do to others, like
> when I hit and punch.—*Jessica*

> I threw away when my mother spanks me.—*Carlos*

> I took all my anger like when my sister takes my money belt and
> hides it and it takes an hour to find it. My balloon was black.
> Black makes garbage. I threw away all my sickness.—*Sean*

Sean continued to use the process of visualization when he went for radiation treatments, and we continued sending him healing energy and love. The love that was shared in that class was extraordinary.

Sean recovered fully, much to the joyful gratitude of his family and all of us. Now, two years later, he can fully engage in sports activities and play team soccer. He has incorporated the imagery process into his life; he still chooses whether to stay with bad feelings and anger or to put them in the balloon and let them go. He and his family use the visualization process in new or fearful situations, and Sean has found a sense of security and confidence in his ability to do something about his feelings. He gave all of us a tremendous gift in teaching us about the power of love.

Imagery gives us a tool to deal with feelings. We can hold on to uncomfortable feelings, including anger, frustration, and pain, or we can use imagery to dissolve them. Children are often told to express how they feel. This, however, is not always easy because negative feelings are often hard to define. Sometimes a person will experience a general overall feeling of discomfort but will be unable to attribute this to any one incident.

It is comforting to know that you can do something about this discomfort. You can image yourself feeling calm and relaxed; envision yourself surrounded by love; and make a choice to release the feelings that prevent you from functioning at your fullest. Or you may find that as you calm and center yourself, you become more aware of what is bothering you and you can do something about it.

Families and classes that use short relaxation and imagery exercises find themselves growing closer. A genuine sense of bonding and caring evolves during the imagery process. Somehow each member of the family or class gains greater insight into their own feelings and those of others. A realization that separateness does not have to exist occurs; we can coexist in understanding and love.

PEACE ON EARTH

What makes imagery such an effective learning and living tool? How does it work? We don't know for certain what part of the brain is involved in imagery, but my own speculation, based upon experience, research, and reading, is that in imagery we engage the most recently evolved part of the human brain—the prefrontal lobes. What is the significance of this? It might just be that in exercising the prefrontal lobes, a new human being is evolving; one who understands the deep meaning and everlasting impact of love and peace.

Paul MacLean, chief of the Laboratory of Brain Evolution and Behavior of the National Institutes of Mental Health, describes the brain as three interconnected brains in one. Each of these brains corresponds to a separate major evolutionary step; the brain has evolved a new, more sophisticated layer as humans became more intelligent, caring beings.

Our "reptile" brain evolved several hundred million years ago and plays an important role in aggressive behavior, territoriality, ritual, and the establishment of social hierarchies. We see some of this behavior exhibited by very young children and institutions.

A new layer, the limbic system, developed 150 million years ago with the evolution of the early mammal. There was a profound shift of consciousness from the laying of eggs to the carrying of the baby in the womb. The limbic system plays an important part in the care of the young. It marks the root of emotions, unity of family and clan, and the ability to play. The limbic system is very important in the development of the adolescent.

The most recent layer, which comprises 85 percent of the human brain, is the neocortex. This evolved as human beings began to use tools and language simultaneously. The neocortex is involved in higher cognitive functioning. One model of cognitive function divides the neocortex into two hemispheres, each specializing in different modes of thinking.

We are just recently beginning to learn about the importance of the prefrontal lobes of the neocortex, the most recently evolved part of the brain. According to MacLean's research, the prefrontals bring heart and a sense of compassion into the world. They are the seat of empathy, altruism, and compassionate identification with another person. We use our prefrontal lobes to plan for the future, to fantasize about how things may turn out, not only for ourselves but for others. MacLean reports that there are clinical indications that the prefrontal cortex helps us to gain insight into the feelings of others.[3]

If we have arrived in our brain development at a point in which we can teach insight, foresight, compassion, and love, there is hope for a more peaceful, harmonious planet. It is possible that we can use guided imagery to envision harmonious living conditions, to send healing energy to those in pain, and to send love to those in need. There is also the possibility that through expanded learning techniques such as guided imagery, we can help our children bring their images into reality.

INSIDE-OUTSIDE

It's like the earth and I are one when the sun is just felt, but not seen. I'm in my own world and the earth is all around and smells sweet. Trust is new and fragrant but going home makes a lost feeling come up within me. I will try and be as a person in the woods, feeling free to share and be all I am. The time of this is so right and I feel so marvelously new!

The universe, the earth, and me.

A connecting rod of hope and light from the earth out into the outer reaches of time and space.

You are so beautiful to me!

You are . . . so beautiful to me!

—*Kristie*

Healing Cells

AGE: 8 through adult
TIME: 5–10 minutes

This exercise may be used with people who have cancer, leukemia, or AIDS.

Close your eyes and begin to focus your attention on your breath. Now all of your attention is on one thing, the air entering and leaving your nostrils. (*Pause*) Know that you have the ability to communicate directly to your physical body with your brain/mind. Today you are going to communicate healing commands to your body. Focus your attention on your heart and become aware of your blood system flowing in and out of your heart and throughout your body and brain. Imagine a vast, powerful army of white healing cells, swimming through your blood system like a school of fish. This school of strong white healing cells cleanses your blood and purifies your immune system. It purifies your organs, your muscles, your bones, your skin and hair, eliminating and flushing out any disease as it travels throughout your body. Feel the powerful healing energy of this school of white healing cells as its swims through your blood system. (*Pause 2 minutes*)

You now experience your body as a strong, healthy organism. In a moment I will count to ten. Join me at the count of six, opening your eyes at ten, feeling relaxed and alert. One . . . two . . . three . . . four . . . five . . . six . . . seven . . . eight . . . nine . . . ten.

KEVIN

EXERCISE 21

Heart Meditation

AGE: 3–12
TIME: 3–5 minutes

Sit in a comfortable position. Close your eyes and focus your attention on your breath, breathing in . . . and . . . out . . . in . . . and . . . out. (*Pause*) Now, as you continue to breathe in a relaxed manner, focus your attention on your heart space in the middle of your chest. (*Pause*) Breathe into your heart and fill your heart with love and energy. (*Pause*) As you continue to breathe, the love energy expands, getting larger and larger, filling your whole chest and possibly your whole body. You may associate some color with this love energy. Now send the love from your heart out into the center of the circle. This unites with the love from everyone else in the room. (*Pause*) And now send that combined love to someone who is not present and who you know needs extra love at this time. (*Pause*) Now bring this love and energy back to yourself, and when you are ready, slowly open your eyes.

RESPONSES TO "HEART MEDITATION"

I sent love and energy to everyone who needs it.—*Jessica*

My hand was warm and got warmer as my heart beat. I sent love and energy to Donna and her baby. When I sent it into the center it was like a waterfall.—*Mary*

I sent love and energy to my cousin who has the flu and wanted to go outside and play but couldn't. I felt energy around me and a zap of energy came from Sean's back.—*John*

I felt tingly. I sent love and energy to Kirsten and a baby I saw on television who's blind in one eye and has a hole in his heart.
—*Chris*

I have a cold so I sent my energy to my nose. Then I sent it to my leg because I hurt it yesterday. It felt like a vibration. My nose felt funny because it was vibrating.—*Sean*

EXERCISE 22
Lotus Flower Meditation

AGE: 3 through adult
TIME: 5 minutes

Close your eyes and focus your attention on your heart or the area in the middle of your chest. Imagine there a closed golden-petaled lotus flower. As you breathe into your heart, the energy from your heart slowly opens the petals of the lotus flower (*pause*) and a beautiful blue light emanates from the center of the lotus flower. You have all the time you need to open your flower. (*Pause 1 minute*) As the lotus continues to open, the blue light expands, filling you with love and light. (*Pause 1 minute*) Notice how the blue light from your heart joins with the light from the hearts here present. (*Pause*) Now let that image go, notice how you feel, and slowly open your eyes, feeling fully alert yet very relaxed.[4]

RESPONSES TO "LOTUS FLOWER MEDITATION"

The flower was yellow and the petals opened two by two. It was like blue lava coming from my heart and the white light came from the sky. When they came together it made sparks. One side of me felt hot and the other side was cold.—*Kevin*

I could see the hostages [in Iran] being freed because the guards were lying around with white and blue light going around them and they let the hostages go.—*Sean*

My flower uncurled one petal at a time and it was all colors. I sent love and energy to everyone who needed it.—*Denise*

I was using soft eyes and I saw your energy coming out of you. My energy hit your energy beam and joined it and both went to Donna [who at that time was in labor with her first child].
—*Carlos*

NOTE TO PARENTS AND TEACHERS

Exercise 23 is a variation of the Power Shield exercise. I adapted it for the Santa Monica–based Thursday Night Group, an educational organization that facilitates peace training for children of all ages.

Provide paper and markers or crayons. Have your children or students draw circles divided into four sections. In them, they will draw pictures or symbols that represent skills or strengths, fears, dreams, and actions needed to bring about their dreams for the future. Emphasize that this exercise is not about artistic ability and does not require good art skills. It is important to make concrete images that have appeared in imagery exercises so that the person can work with them. Discuss the shields after they have been drawn.

Emphasize that each person makes a difference in life and it is important for children and adolescents to realize that what they dream for the future can come true if they are willing to use their skills, address their fears and come to terms with them, and see the options they have to create a healthy life for themselves and their loved ones.

Peace Shield

AGE: 9–18
EXERCISE: 10–15 minutes
FOLLOW-UP: 15–30 minutes

Since we know that action follows thought, it is important to realize that each one of us is responsible for our thoughts and our actions about the future of the planet. The future depends upon you, your thoughts, your dreams, your actions.

It is important to think about what strengths and skills you bring to the present as well as to the future. It is also important to know what fears you might carry because they can influence how you see yourself participating in changing the future. If you are afraid, it is hard to think about changing what you might be afraid of. It also helps to know what wishes and dreams you have for yourself and your family and friends, and what actions you will have to take to make those dreams come true.

Today we are going to make a personal power shield that shows who we are. In many cultures, including European and American Indian, families have shields or crests that say something about them, their strengths, their animal totem, perhaps their name. Your shield will be divided up into four quadrants, in which you will draw your (1) strengths or skills, (2) fears, (3) dreams for the future, and (4)actions required by you to achieve your dreams.

Close your eyes and sit in a comfortable position. Focus your attention on your breath, and as you exhale release any tension that you may be storing in your body. Give yourself the suggestion that with each exhalation your body becomes more and more relaxed. (*Pause*)

Good. Now continue to breathe at your own rate and focus on a point in the middle of your forehead between your closed eyes. Imagine a circle in this spot that slowly begins to expand with each breath that you take. As you continue to breathe, your circle begins to grow and grow, getting larger and larger, until you and the circle are one. (*Pause*)

Now in your circle you begin to see, sense, or feel images that represent your skills and abilities. These may be actual physical or mental skills, artistic or musical skills, or communications skills. Notice what makes you feel good about who you are as a person. (*Pause 1 minute*)

Now begin to see, sense, or image your fears. Whether these are small fears or large ones, you are perfectly safe here at the present time. These may be obstacles that you are facing in your life at the present or fears that you have about the future. (*Pause 1 minute*)

Now you begin to see, sense, or imagine your dreams for yourself and loved ones for the future. How is it that you want to live your life? (*Pause 1 minute*)

Now in the last part of the circle you begin to see, sense, or imagine what you and others will do to realize your dreams. What action will you take? (*Pause 1 minute*)

In a moment I will count to ten. Please join me counting aloud at the count of six, opening your eyes at ten, ready to draw the pictures from your imagination about your skills, fears, dreams, and the action necessary to make your dreams come true. One . . . two . . . three . . . four . . . five . . . six . . . seven . . . eight . . . nine . . . ten.

TEN

Entering Adolescence

◎ ◎ ◎ ◎ ◎ ◎ ◎

Puberty is a period of being cast out from the "secret garden" of childhood. The emerging adolescent is a totally different being from what he or she was before sexual maturity. Adolescents have to face the external world in a way they have never had to before. It is miraculous that so many people survive adolescence intact!

The physical, emotional, mental, and spiritual changes that accompany adolescence bring anxiety for both the child and parents or teachers. During the teenage years (approximately 10–19) the child has to address specific stressors that pertain to self-concept, body image, emotions, friendship, peer pressures, parental expectations for grades and behavior, time and money pressures, sexual identity, moving away from the safety of home into the unknown world of adulthood, and fears about death.

These stressors are present whether you live in a rural environment or in the city, and they must be dealt with or the adolescent experiences anger, depression, headaches, stomache aches, eating disorders, or sleep problems, or begins to abuse substances such as alcohol, cigarettes, or drugs. By keeping the lines of communication open between parents/teachers and adolescents and by using imagery exercises as a tool to reduce stress, this transition from childhood to adulthood can be made smoother.

FITTING IN

Junior high brings with it not only a move to a new school but a period of experimentation—trying out new friends, new clothes, new music, new language, and new hairstyles. Friends become a priority for many adolescents, and the desire to belong to a group becomes a need.

Abraham Maslow, one of the founders of humanistic psychology, studied what people need in their lives and developed the concept of a hierarchy of needs, as illustrated on the next page.

SHIP VIA	# OF CARTONS	SHIP DATE
UPS		

RIPTION	PRICE	AMOUNT
	14.95	14.95
RD		3.50
		0.75
ND HANDLING		19.20
OICE AMOUNT		19.20CR
ID		0.00
AID		

for your order ***

PLEASE PAY LAST
AMOUNT SHOWN

ASH

INVOICE

TELE: (617)

SHAMBHALA PUBLICATIONS
300 MASSACHUSETTS AVE
BOSTON,MA   02115

```
S
O   T
L   O
D
```

DR.PETER KEVORKIAN
435 HIGH ST
WESTWOOD, MA 02090

BOOKS: Special 4th class rate
forwarding & return postage guaranteed

INVOICE NO.:	DATE	ACCOUNT NUMBER	
K177001-89	11-17-87	02090KEVORP.1	

QUANTITY	BACK ORDER	ISBN PREFIX 0-87773	DESC
1		422	(SP) SPINNING INWA
			POSTAGE AN
			TAX
			TOTAL INV
			AMOUNT PA
			INVOICE P
			*** Thank you

1987 NOV 18 AM 8:00

1743

TELE: (617) 424-0030   TERMS: C

Self-Actualization
Self-Esteem
Love and Belongingness
Safety and Security Needs
Basic Physiological Needs

The most basic needs are for water, food, shelter, warmth, sleep, activity, movement, and sex. Second is the need to be safe from harm. Third is the need to feel loved and cared for by family, friends, or some other group. Fourth is the need for esteem, approval, dignity, and self-respect. At the highest level is the need for self-actualization: knowing who you are, being everything you can be, and being creative.[1]

Putting Maslow's ideas into vastly simplified terms, we can say that we have to satisfy the most basic need before we can go on to meet the next level of need. If we are starving or freezing, we don't think about our safety. If we don't feel safe, we don't care much about belonging. If we don't feel loved or cared for, we don't think about liking ourselves. And if we don't like ourselves, we can't be creative and reach our full potential.

Sometimes needs change very quickly. If a teenager's boyfriend breaks up with her, she only thinks about belonging. If someone in the group she has just joined talks about her behind her back, she feels betrayed or ostracized. Teenagers can be insensitive about each other's feelings in their desperate need to belong.

Your teenager may wish to talk with you about difficulties with friends. Remember not to trivialize these relationships or the hurts that accompany disappointment in friendship. Adolescents need to examine what is important to them about certain friendships, how they can reach out to make new friends, and how to deal with friends of the opposite sex.

I led my eighth-grade class in an imagery exercise that is an excellent warmup for a discussion on friendship. In the exercise they choose a friend to take to a desert island, noticing what they value about this friendship as the two of them explore the island. The following responses reflect what they valued about their friend:

> He shares the same interests as I, the same humor.
> My friend and I work together well—we both love camping
> and art.
> He is someone I can make mistakes with, someone I can be to-
> tally open with about my disappointments.

115

I can share my dreams for the future with her.
She doesn't let me get away with fooling myself about what I'm doing.
He makes me think.
She's willing to make mistakes in front of me.

Exploring the concept of friendship through imagery can help adolescents make choices about the type of people they want in their lives. The following response by a fifteen-year-old girl makes this clear.

> I took Jill to Puntarenas, Costa Rica. The light is beautiful here and she likes to paint so I knew we could spend our days painting and taking photographs. We both enjoy the people and the food in the cantinas and enjoy hiking in the mountains. Jill is afraid of heights so we have to climb the trails slowly but I don't mind because it gives me time to photograph and enjoy the colors of the foliage.
>
> One of the things I value about Jill is that she always tells me the truth, even if it is hard for me to hear—the truth about myself, about what she does and does not like about me and the way I am with her. She is someone I can share my disappointments with as well as my joys. She makes me think in new ways because we don't look at things the same way. We don't always agree and that's positive.
>
> I can be totally myself with her which includes being very silly. We laugh a lot together.

SELF-CONCEPT IN ADOLESCENCE

Parents and family have been the most important people in a child's life, and they have the most important role in forming the child's self-concept—until adolescence. During the teenage years, friends seem to take the preeminent role in determining the child's self-concept. Teachers and other adults, including coaches and bosses, become important as well. In the end, the child is the one who decides what she thinks of herself, but she uses other people to "measure" herself and as models for how she should be.

Unfortunately, many early adolescents (age 12–14) who compare themselves with others concentrate only on their weaknesses instead of their strengths. They look at what they don't have—good grades, popularity, an attractive appearance—instead of what they do have. They may develop unrealistic expectations of themselves, their friends, or their parents and begin to focus on the negative.

Your job as a parent or teacher is to help them see the positive aspects of themselves and to help them sort through their confusion about applying the specific to the general. Sometimes people think that when one thing goes wrong, then everything is bad. For example, a boy who doesn't make the team may think that he is no good. Children forget that everyone fails, gets angry, does better than others at some things, and goes through cycles of growth and decline throughout life. You need to help them gain perspective.

A healthy self-concept exists when we accept who we are, *exactly* the way we are, and feel that we are important in life. Our society is afflicted with the illness of "not enough," and our teenagers are suffering the consequences of it. "I didn't get enough work done . . . a high enough grade . . . enough awards . . . enough money . . . enough friends . . . enough sex/food/clothes/ creature comforts/recognition. . . ." This type of thinking undermines the growth of healthy self-esteem. It sets up a pattern of dissatisfaction with self because the underlying message is "I am not enough."

We *are* enough, and it is our job as educators and parents to help our children feel safe and secure in who they are. You can help teenagers build their self-esteem by guiding them to concentrate on the skills and talents they have instead of longing to be someone else. Encourage them to notice every time they do something successful, and teach them to view mistakes as a way to learn rather than as a defeat. Assist them to clarify goals and to visualize themselves as successful in whatever they want to do. The clearer the picture, the better the chance they have of building a positive self-image. "Accepting Myself" (Exercise 26) is an excellent imagery exercise to build self-esteem and healthy attitudes that will shape the direction of a teenager's life.

UNPREDICTABLE MOODS

For all ages, exercises that develop concentration, creativity, and intuitive thinking are important, but an added emphasis for older children is to give them an active understanding of the functioning of their emotions, brain, and physical body. Teenagers are flooded with emotions they don't understand. In early adolescence they experience wide mood swings; one moment they feel happy and the next they feel sad.

As thirteen-year-old Amy explained, "Sometimes my feelings make me cry for no reason or maybe I'll get angry at someone for nothing. These mood changes are scary because I can't control my feelings." Some people become more irritable and argue more often during adolescence. "When

I'm in a bad mood I tune people out and just don't listen to what others, particularly my parents or teachers, are saying to me," says fourteen-year-old Craig. "I just pick on my mother and then I feel better," says fifteen-year-old Eddie.

Unless teenagers have a healthy way to release these unpredictable feelings, a parent, sibling, or teacher will pay the price. Emotions get stored in the body as muscle tension, headaches, stomach aches, and fatigue. You can help your adolescent release them with stress reduction exercises such as "Clearing Space" (Exercise 27) and "Wave" (Exercise 29).

BODY IMAGE

The physical changes that occur during adolescence can be a major cause of stress for a teenager. Girls worry about getting taller than the boys around them, how big or small their breasts are, and when they are going to menstruate. Boys worry about penis size, their voice cracking, and if they are ever going to grow taller. Both boys and girls worry about their looks, weight, facial structure, body hair, and pimples.

Girls may hear statements from their fathers like, "Oh, dear, it's too bad you've got your mother's thighs," or boys may be told by their mothers, "Your father didn't grow until he was nineteen." Such comments, although said to humor or reassure, can be the kiss of death to sensitive teenagers, who already feel betrayed by their bodies. Be careful not to trivialize their concern by making genetic jokes and perpetuating family myths. Help them to realize that they may carry negative images about themselves in their bodies and that they have a choice to change those images to positive ones.

Many adolescents may store feelings of inadequacy and self-loathing in their bodies as well as tension about school performance and social relationships. Dr. Eugene Gendlin and his associates at the University of Chicago have developed a technique that teaches people how to identify and change the way personal problems and attitudes concretely exist in the body. He calls the technique "focusing."

Focusing is a process in which one makes contact with a special kind of internal bodily awareness, called a felt sense. A felt sense is the body's sense of a particular problem or situation that is not recognizable at first. This vague feeling is described by many adolescents as being "out of synch." As these subtle sensations come into focus, the body finds its own way to provide answers to unspoken problems.[2]

An example of this is the constant pressure adolescents feel to conform to the media's image of beauty and sexuality. Despite intense lobbying during the last twenty years to eliminate stereotypical images of women and minorities, sexism and racism still exist. In fact, exploitation of sex and race has become a lucrative tool for the advertising industry.

After doing the exercise "Clearing Space," seventeen-year-old Luisah wrote:

> Since I was a girl I have been bombarded with media images
> and messages that say a black woman can't be beautiful so I told
> myself that being beautiful didn't matter. I just have to work
> hard. But I know now that I am strong and that I don't have to be
> white and blond to matter in this life. I know that I'm beautiful.

THE BRAIN IN ADOLESCENCE

Research on the human brain cannot give us answers yet on how best to educate our students, but it can provide useful analogies, revise old theories, suggest new hypotheses, and eliminate some old ideas about teaching and learning.

We don't all learn in the same way, and we don't learn the same material well at the same chronological age. Sex does affect learning, brain structure does affect learning, hormones do affect learning and behavior. How we feel about ourselves affects how well we learn and remember. People learn and remember different things from the same event, depending on the organizational processes they use.

Research carried out by Herman Epstein has found that the brain, like all other organs, grows in a stagewise fashion and has both periods of rapid growth (during ages 2–4, 6–8, 10–12, and 14–16) and plateaus (during ages 4–6, 8–10, and 12–14) where there is virtually no significant brain growth or increase in number of synapses. This does not mean that there is new cell formation in the brain during growth spurts, but rather that more synaptic connections are made during these times of growth. And these differ between boys and girls.

During the 10–12 growth spurt, female brain growth is about three times that of males, while the situation is reversed, favoring males, during the 14–16 brain growth period. So girls need a more challenging curriculum than boys from ages 10 to 12 and a less intense and complex one at 15. There often occurs a "turn-off" of achievement because of overchallenge. Many courses involving "formal operations" begin at 14 (ninth grade) when readiness is not there because the child is in a plateau period. During plateau periods, the child should be exposed to large amounts of information and a wide variety of *direct* experience with nature, science, people, and work all from the point of view of enlarging the direct experience base.[3]

Teachers and parents have the responsibility during adolescence to facilitate attention, ask questions where connections can be made, and provide experiences with the "real world."

Parents also need to remember not to put *unreasonable* demands on teenagers for grades. I hear comments like "My mother will *kill* me if I don't get into Harvard" or "My father will never forgive me if I don't do well in chemistry. He just doesn't understand that I'm not a science whiz like him."

Help your children or students become actively aware of working with their brain and memory, and help them to manage their time to create effective study skills. Use "Brain As a Retrieval System" (Exercise 28) to help adolescents prepare mentally for a test. Don't create more stress in their lives by wanting them to succeed where you did or didn't. Let them live their own lives, make their own mistakes, and learn how to make the best choices for themselves.

USING GUIDED IMAGERY EXERCISES WITH ADOLESCENTS

Adolescents need to understand *why* you want them to do anything. It is no good appealing to the sense of adult authority that they had when they were younger. Now they demand to know reasons for whatever they are expected to do.

Guided imagery exercises *do* reduce stress, help a person to relax, and clear the mind of static and chatter. When I first introduced guided imagery to my twelfth-grade Human Development class, seventeen-year-old Alexandra commented:

> I find it very difficult to experience guided imagery completely because I am such a tense person. I need to be alert so often during the day that it is almost impossible to participate and let myself go. I find myself too often thinking about something that just happened or something that will happen. It is my tendency to think so much that causes me the greatest pain and the greatest joy. My feet, back, neck, hands and face held extreme tension when we started. I did experience a release of tension in my back when you took us to the beach.

Experience is the best teacher when it comes to guided imagery. You may meet resistance when you first introduce these exercises at home or in the classroom, but if you respect your adolescents' need for privacy and safety and accept their feelings, you will have more success. I usually find that it takes at least four to six sessions for them to get used to the newness of this technique. Be careful of your expectations.

Teenagers may not want to share much verbally about their experience of the exercises. Give them time to make concrete their images in writing, drawing, watercolor, or clay. You may wish to suggest an Imagery Journal in which they can keep a record of their images. The more they work with imagery, the more often images recur and expand.

IN THE CLASSROOM

If you have a typical junior or senior high school classroom, you probably have desks or tables that are not easy to move and a time limit of forty-five to fifty minutes with your students. I do not have my own classroom but move from room to room throughout the school building. The first thing I have my students do with me as they enter the room is to push desks and tables against the wall. We then sit in a circle either on chairs or on the floor. Often, my students lie on the floor if there is a rug or if they have brought a towel or mat. If the desktop is attached to the chair, many students may choose to put their head down on the desk. We light a candle in the middle of the circle and often put a crystal there as well. I turn out the lights and play soft, relaxing music as I begin the imagery exercise. Some students do not actually close their eyes but enjoy the restful quiet of the semidark room.

After we finish the exercise, I give them time to write or draw their experience and then share it verbally if they choose. Older adolescents are more private about their thoughts, feelings, and fantasies than younger children and are often afraid of how they will be perceived by their peers. The following response by Andy, age seventeen, illustrates his resistance, his fear of being judged, and how he resolved his feelings.

> I was very resistant and did not feel comfortable closing my eyes or lying down so I just stayed alert and thought about stuff. I remember liking having my eyes open when it was dark. It felt good to my eyes. My leg brace was uncomfortable and my leg hurt. I wanted to move around and whisper something to someone who really likes me but I don't have any close friends in class. I wanted to be like John Wayne but I thought that everybody would think that I was a jerk. Bonnie looked pretty with her eyes closed, like a painting. I liked watching people. I felt powerful. I remembered catching my first wave over the summer on a surfboard.

When the bell rings at the end of the period we quickly put the room back together for the next teacher. It is not an ideal situation, but it works. Teachers who have their own homeroom often use pillows and incense. I meet with each class for a fifty-minute period twice a week, and we use imagery once every four meetings. It is not as much time as I would like, but it is consistent and the exercises have value. My students look forward to a time when they can relax and "come home to themselves."

Teachers often ask me how to lead the exercise. I lead the exercises with my eyes closed because I am comfortable doing so. I can also participate in this way. This is my style, but it may not be comfortable for others. Many teachers read the exercises directly from the book, being mindful of pacing their reading. Other teachers prefer to make tapes of their own voice or use commercially made tapes. Use the method that works for you and experiment. There is no *right* way in imaging.

AT HOME

Each family has to work out its own schedule for practicing guided imagery together. Sunday morning works with my family, though not on a weekly basis. As children get older, they spend more and more time away from the family with friends, sports, and other activities. This is one of the reasons why it is important to start practicing guided imagery when children are young. They can then continue these exercises on their own as they get older, particularly in times of confusion or when they need guidance.

I had the rewarding experience of teaching Katya guided imagery in kindergarten and then, twelve years later, taking her on a senior-class retreat. She told me that the exposure she had with guided imagery as a young child had allowed her to maintain a strong connection to her dream symbols as well as the spiritual dimension of her life. Her present meditation practice grew out of her earlier experience.

Suggest to your adolescents or class that they write about or draw their experiences of Exercise 24, paying particular attention to the details of the island environment and to their relationship with their friend. Why did they choose this person, and what do they value about this friendship? What do they learn about themselves when they are with this person? Do they act differently with this friend than they do with others? This exercise can be used to begin a discussion on friendship.

Friendship on a Desert Island

AGE: 11–17
EXERCISE: 5 minutes
FOLLOW-UP: 15–20 minutes

In this exercise you will choose a friend to go with you to explore a deserted island. Notice what it is about this friendship that you value.

Close your eyes and focus your attention on your breath. Now take three deep breaths, releasing any tension that you carry in your body as you breathe out. (*Pause*) Good. Now give yourself the suggestion that with each exhalation your body becomes more and more relaxed.

Imagine that you are traveling through space and time, with a friend of your own choosing, to a deserted island. The two of you arrive and begin to explore this island, noticing its vegetation, animal and bird life, climate, smells, colors, textures, and tastes. You have chosen this friend to accompany you for a particular reason. What is it about this person that you like? Notice how you interact with this person. Notice what it is about this friendship that you value. You will have three minutes of clock time equal to all of the time that you need to explore this island together. Begin. (*Pause 3 minutes*)

Now take one last look around the island before you leave, noticing the colors, smells, sounds, and textures. (*Pause*)

Now gently bring your attention back into this room. In a moment I will count to ten. Join me at the count of six, opening your eyes at ten, feeling refreshed and alert and with full memory of your experience. One . . . two . . . three . . . four . . . five . . . six . . . seven . . . eight . . . nine . . . ten.

EXERCISE 25
Mirror Reflection

AGE: 10–15
TIME: 10 minutes

Close your eyes and begin to focus your attention on your breath, so that all of your attention is on the air flowing in . . . and . . . out of your nostrils. As you breathe, give yourself the suggestion that with each exhalation your body becomes more and more relaxed. (*Pause*)

Now imagine that you are walking along in a lush green forest and you see a house on a hill in the distance. You approach the house and the doors are open, so you go inside. You find yourself in a large room where the walls, ceiling, and floor are made of mirrors. Music begins to play, and you listen carefully to the music, which you recognize. You approach one of the mirrored walls, looking at your reflection, and all of a sudden your reflection begins to dance to the music. You join in, following the lead of your partner, who is yourself. You have three minutes of clock time equal to all of the time you need to experience this dance. (*Pause 3 minutes*)

Now bring your dance to a close, leave your partner, and come back here, with full memory of your movement and of what you learned about your reflection. I will count to ten. Please join me at the count of six and open your eyes at ten, feeling relaxed and alert. One . . . two . . . three . . . four . . . five . . . six . . . seven . . . eight . . . nine . . . ten.

NOTE: This imagery exercise usually evokes the sound of music for most people who participate. If this is not the case, you may wish to play "Spring" from Vivaldi's *The Four Seasons,* starting the record or tape when you get to the exercise directions "Music begins to play."

I Am a Hero

A wonderful feeling of love
Came to me today,
And I follow it.
And I am no longer me,
I am a spirit, a wise being from
deep inside my soul.

And I am love itself
I am generosity,
I am a tree, a blade of grass
I am the sun, the moon, the
stars.
I am bravery.

And I find a hero within
myself.
I am a hero.

MARIA

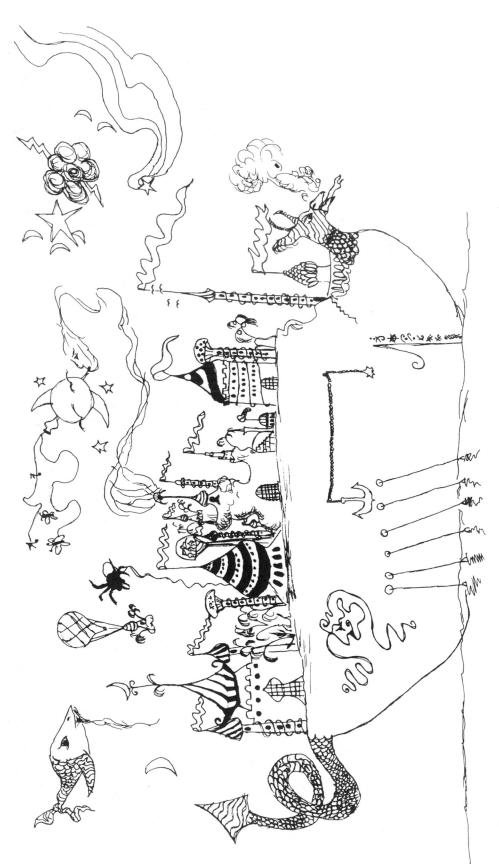

DREW

EXERCISE 26
Accepting Myself

AGE: 13–18
EXERCISE: 5–10 minutes
FOLLOW-UP: 10–15 minutes

Close your eyes and focus your attention on your breath. As you breathe in . . . and out . . . gently through your nose or mouth, allow yourself to become more and more relaxed. As you gently breathe in . . . and . . . out, your feet become relaxed (*pause*), your legs become relaxed (*pause*), your abdomen becomes relaxed (*pause*), your back and shoulders become relaxed (*pause*), and your arms and hands become relaxed (*pause*). And as you continue to breathe in . . . and . . . out, gently and quietly, your head becomes relaxed and your mind floats free. You find yourself floating away from this room to a place where you feel really good. It may be a place in nature, a place you have visited on vacation, anywhere where you feel good about yourself. When you get there, just enjoy being there. Enjoy the warmth of the sun . . . and breathe it into yourself. Feel the warmth of the sun and feel filled with love. Now see yourself as perfect exactly the way you are . . . as a friend (*pause*) . . . with your family (*pause*) . . . with yourself. See yourself at ease with something that you enjoy doing, whether it is soccer, ice skating, playing piano, drawing, singing, conversing with friends, or being alone. Just experience the joy of being you. (*Pause*) Continue to feel the warmth of the sun and to breathe in a feeling of peace and well-being. (*Pause 2 minutes*)

Now I am going to call you back. Bring this feeling of well-being with you, and carry it with you throughout the day. I will count to three. Open your eyes at the count of three, ready to draw or write about your experience. One . . . two . . . three.

EXERCISE 27

Clearing Space

AGE: 13 through adult
TIME: 15–20 minutes

Close your eyes and begin to focus your attention on your breath. Notice the air moving in and out of your nostrils, and notice your breath rate—is it shallow or deep, long or short? Focus all of your attention on your breath. (*Pause*) In a moment, but not yet, I will ask you to take inventory of your body, noticing where it is that you carry tension or discomfort. Your task is to focus on each area that I suggest, noticing how it feels. We will start with the feet.

Shift your attention to your feet and bring your feet into your awareness. Are you aware of any sensations in your feet? Are they relaxed . . . Tired? . . . Notice how they feel. (*Pause*)

Now gently shift your attention to your legs, becoming aware of your calves, knees, and thighs, noticing if you carry any tension or discomfort in your legs. (*Pause*)

Now gently shift your attention to your genital area and buttocks, noticing any sensations or tension that you carry in that area. (*Pause*)

Bring your attention now to your stomach and solar plexus, becoming aware of any tension or discomfort that you may carry in that area. (*Pause*)

Become aware of your chest and notice any tightness or discomfort you may experience. (*Pause*)

Shift your attention to your back and shoulders, noticing any tension or discomfort you may carry. (*Pause*)

Now bring your awareness into your arms, elbows, wrists, and hands, noticing if you hold any tension in your arms and hands. (*Pause*)

Focus your attention now on your neck and jaw, noticing if you hold any frustration, anger, or tension in this area. (*Pause*)

Bring your awareness into your facial muscles, forehead, and head, noticing if you carry any tightness or discomfort in your head. (*Pause*)

Now that you have taken inventory of your entire body, choose one area to focus on where you carry tension or discomfort. (*Pause*) Good.

Now create a box of your own design where you can dispose of all the images, words, people, memories, attitudes, and expectations that are stored in your body. Place it next to you. (*Pause*) Now silently, to yourself,

130

say, "I could feel perfectly OK at the present time if it were not for . . ." and let each image, word, person, memory, expectation that is stored in your body begin to emerge one by one. As each image appears, put it into the box without censorship or explanation. Continue to do so until you make space for yourself. Begin. "I could feel perfectly OK at the present time if it were not for . . ." (*Pause 3 minutes*) Now put the lid on the box and ask an ally or guide to come and dispose of the box and its contents in a way that is healing to the earth. (*Pause*) Once again focus your attention on your body and notice how you feel. Notice if you have been able to make space for yourself. Enjoy that sensation. (*Pause 1 minute*) Now I will count to ten. Gently start to bring yourself back to full waking consciousness. Join me at the count of six, opening your eyes at ten, feeling relaxed and alert.[4]

EXERCISE 28

The Brain As a Retrieval System

AGE: 12 through adult
TIME: 3–5 minutes

Students can use this exercise when studying for a test. It is a tool for working with memory.

Close your eyes and focus your attention on your breath. Give yourself the suggestion that with each exhalation your body becomes more and more relaxed. (*Pause*)

Now bring your attention up to your brain and become aware of the weight, the size, and the creativity of your brain. Imagine your brain as the intricate, complex organism that it is, pulsing with information. (*Pause*) In your brain is stored everything that you have ever heard, read, studied, seen, done, or felt. All you have to do is to suggest to your brain that you remember everything that is necessary to succeed on this test. You can look into the file where you have stored the subject you will be tested on. You will understand fully everything that you find in the file, and you will be able to use this information and for the benefit of others. Take the next minute to begin a dialogue with your brain. (*Pause 1 minute*)

Now I will count to five. Open your eyes at five, feeling relaxed and alert and with full memory of the contents of your brain. One . . . two . . . three . . . four . . . five.

ELEVEN

The Quest for Identity

In this society we have few rituals to mark the end of childhood and the beginning of adulthood. We want our teenagers to take more and more responsibility for their lives as they choose jobs, girlfriends or boyfriends, and colleges, but we still treat them like kids. We punish them by withholding privileges if we think they are not behaving like responsible adults.

Teenagers are beginners. They are facing many adult experiences and problems for the first time. All of a sudden they are confronted with issues as diverse as the meaning of male and female roles, sexual identity and sexual activity, financial worries, car insurance, applying for jobs, decisions about college and leaving home, and trying to figure out who they are. In addition, we still want them to take out the trash and get every assignment in on time. They need all of our understanding, guidance, patience, and encouragement, and of course we also want their cooperation and respect. What usually ensues is an emotional tug of war.

To find their own identity, adolescents often reject parental and other authority figures and rely on their friends for support and solace. In older adolescence (16–19) the search for one's true identity intensifies. This very search is what frightens parents and teachers and makes them more restrictive.

The adolescent faces the need to assert her will to know her own identity and her fear that if she does so she will lose her parents' love. The underlying message is, "Can I risk asserting who I am, or do I have to conform to be loved by you?" As seventeen-year-old Brett says, "I wish my dad would understand that I'm only young once and I need to experiment. I'm not trying to make him mad. I just need to explore."

Other teens feel guilt about the dichotomy between the self that they show their parents and teachers and the self that is exploring different roles with friends. Eighteen-year-old Tim says, "I wish my parents knew who I really am. They think that I'm so good." Parents are just as confused as

their children. One moment we are holding on, and the next we can't wait to let go.

I watched myself become a more and more restrictive parent as my son prepared to leave for college. During his senior year in high school I tried to enforce earlier and earlier curfews until Brendan pointed out that he had been able to stay out later in ninth grade! I then realized that I was apprehensive not only about what behaviors he and his friends were trying on for size but also about his growing up and moving away from the family.

Saying goodbye to a dependent relationship and trying to find a new way to relate based on independence are the task of the older adolescent as well as the task of the parent or teacher. And it is not easy. This is a period of many mixed emotions. For children, the joy, expectations, and freedom they associate with moving into adulthood are mixed with the fear of leaving the safety and security of the home. Parents wonder whether they have instilled all the "right" values and prepared their son or daughter well enough for life. Teachers worry if they have prepared the student adequately for future study or the workplace. Parents and teachers also have to deal with feelings of loss as the adolescent matures and moves out of their everyday life.

This is a difficult period for the adult who is not conscious of the necessary distancing the adolescent must go through. Adults may often feel rejected, helpless, and unloved and wonder what has happened to the loving relationship that existed between child and adult. Remember that this is a necessary phase of development and will not last forever. The more space you give children to find their own identity, the more they will want to share themselves with you—in time.

STEPPING BACK FROM OVERIDENTIFICATION

Teenagers often become consumed by one thing or another, putting on blinders to anything outside their particular passion. This could be music, fashion, the opposite sex, body image, athletics, or a belief system. There is nothing wrong with this in itself. In fact, it can be quite positive. If we identify with truth, we integrate that quality into our life. It can, however, block the possibility and availability of any other feeling, sensation, or thought when taken to the extreme.[1]

Adolescents cling tenaciously to their identity, how they see themselves and how they wish to be seen by others. At times the intensity of their feelings and ideas causes them to be perceived in a very limited view not only by themselves but by others. We need to teach them how to step back and gain perspective about themselves. An exercise that is helpful in this regard is "Sanctuary" (Exercise 30). It gives young people the opportunity to shift gears, go to a place within that is safe and free from the intensity of teenage feelings, and find a quiet center, a sense of inner peace.

Seventeen-year-old Alex writes:

> I went to the maze at Ojai and looked out at the valley and the ocean, which is always a source of calm for me. It seemed near because of its massiveness, and from far off, its hugeness and calmness soothe me. I had a hard time finding this place. At first I chose my room but there were too many distractions. Then I returned to the site of a great dream I had last night, but I couldn't do any original thinking there because my mind kept wandering back to my dream. I noticed the autumn wind and smelled the trees.

Another exercise that helps one recognize feelings and express them instead of becoming overidentified with them is called the Weather Report. Have your child or students draw a large circle and divide it into four quarters. Ask them how they are feeling right now—mentally, emotionally, and physically. They then write one feeling in each of the four quadrants, and choose two or more feelings to explain.

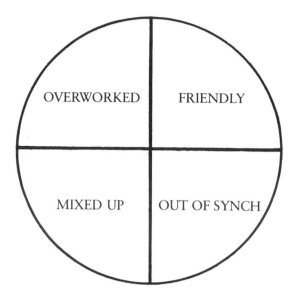

At the bottom of the paper they write "I feel ——— because . . . ," explaining how or why they feel as they do. An example from sixteen-year-old David follows:

> I feel overworked because if I want to get enough sleep I don't get all my schoolwork done. And my personal relationships suffer because I don't have time for them.
>
> I feel mixed up because my sister is coming home. The last time I saw her I realized a lot of negative things about our relationship and I don't want to fall into that again.
>
> I feel friendly because this year I have made new friends. People like me and accept me more than I expect them to. I'm happy.
>
> I feel out of synch with myself because my body is so full of sexual energy I don't know what to do.

Expressing these feelings helps your adolescent accept them, contain them, and understand them so that they no longer run his life. It also helps him to see that he may have conflicting feelings at one time. David felt friendly yet at the same time felt mixed up about his feelings about his sister. Identifying feelings lessens their control over our behavior.

THE SEARCH FOR MEANING

Adolescents experience tremendous pain with the state of affairs in the world and resent their elders for getting us into the mess we're in. Often they experience an existential crisis and express it in despair. "What is life for? What's the point? It doesn't really matter what I do, we're going to get blown up anyway."

I worked as a counselor with teenage drug abusers during the period in our history when both Bobby Kennedy and Martin Luther King, Jr., were assassinated. I was deeply touched by the kids' response to these deaths and to their feeling that life was out of control and that they couldn't do anything about it. "What difference does it make if I stop using drugs when people like Martin Luther King, who are trying so hard to make things better for the people, get killed? What chance do I have of making an impact on the world?"

Our job as parents and educators is to give our children an appreciation of the positive potential in life and to give them the hope that they can effect change. Many older adolescents begin to question their relationship and responsibility to the universe and mistrust the whims of life circumstances beyond their control. They pose questions like, "Is our destiny controlled by some outside force, or do we have control of it?" "Is the Universe something we should be afraid of?" "Is there a Spirit, a Deity, or an external Source, and what effect does it have on our lives?"

These existential questions of adolescence may be addressed by looking at what is beyond our "little local selves" to the transpersonal realm. This includes a search for meaning, a search for value, and a deeper connection to the authentic self.

This exploration of self may be experienced as a feeling of "oneness" with nature or with other living beings. I have heard members of my senior class describe it this way: "When my mask comes off, my guard comes down and I realize that you and I are one. There is no separation; you have the same fears, the same wants, and the same needs that I do."

It is described by runners or skiers as a "peak experience" when they become one with their environment and movement becomes effortless. This visceral realization that the environment and the self work together in harmony is a powerful deterrent to the future abuse of nature or of other living beings and encourages the development of a planetary consciousness. As John Muir said, "If you pull up a flower, you discover that it is connected to everything in the Universe."

The search for a deeper connection to self helps older adolescents to realize their own inner wisdom and recognize that they have all the answers within if they take the time to center, quiet the mind, and listen. The "Ally Within" (Exercise 16) encourages the participant to find a wise being within who gives guidance and support and who may have answers to personal

137

questions. The following is a reponse by Erinn, age seventeen, to this exercise.

> My spirit was more of a feeling, a protection that surrounded me. It led me into the cave surrounded by crystals and I felt a very intense feeling. Tears were falling down my face as though I was letting go. I wanted to hold my spirit, seeking comfort, but my spirit wasn't an object though I could feel it. Needing something to hold on to for security, I reached for a crystal and held it, feeling that my spirit had given a part of himself to my crystal. My spirit told me to let go of my fears of incompetence. He told me that I had a false image of who I was, that I was really much stronger than I believed. He also told me that I should stand up to my mother and yell at her because I was always giving instead of receiving. I am the mother of my mother and my brother, and my spirit told me that I held too much responsibility. He told me that I needed to act like a child once in a while to release tension.

This type of inner dialogue may help participants release tension, gain a new sense of self-confidence and self-acceptance, and realize that they are not alone in the world. It may also give the adolescent a concrete experience of the transcendent realm and a starting point to begin deeper explorations. Eighteen-year-old Matt wrote:

> Meeting my ally affected me deeply; where I hadn't given a consideration to his possibility before, I am now on my way to believing. I may not believe in an outer power, but I do believe in the consciousness of this whole, beautiful organism we call Mother Earth. It touches me, and I plan to follow it up. To leave it hanging now would be to do my ally and myself an injustice.

THE INNER CHILD MEETS THE EXTENDED SELF

Before taking leave of adolescence and leaping with blind faith into adulthood, it is helpful to make contact with the inner child to understand our continuity with and responsibility to the future. We remember who we are when we have the opportunity to relive the love and acceptance we experienced as a child or the lack thereof. Knowing where we have come from helps us choose where we are going, and through guided imagery we may heal any disabling behavior that took its root in early childhood.

"The Inner Child" (Exercise 32) may remind adolescents of the mystery, wonder, and beauty of life and the curiosity, freedom, and creativity of childhood. A dream from the past may be rekindled, a relationship may be understood and healed, an obstacle in the personality may present itself for resolution. To realize our full potential, each of us must come to terms with and learn from the past and appreciate how each part of our personal history influences our collective present and future.

We are more than our bodies, minds, and emotions, our personal needs, wants, and dreams. We have a higher and transcendent nature, and we are part of a species that is slowly evolving toward wholeness. The young child is not separated from this transcendent self, but the adolescent, in pursuit of the rational and intellectual knowledge of the world, becomes split off from his or her spiritual nature. Guided imagery gives teenagers an important opportunity to heal the dichotomy between mind and heart.

It is possible to take a glimpse into the future, to perceive a sense of one's place in the whole through contact with the extended self. The extended self is that part of self which has already reached its full potential, the blueprint that has been actualized. Doing "The Extended Self" (Exercise 33) may produce an insight that may change adolescents' attitudes about themselves and the world around them. They may thereafter see reality in a different way, value life from a new perspective, and lose fear about the future.

My own visit with my extended self has been a source of beauty, inspiration, and strength, particularly during periods of self-doubt.

An old woman came toward me smiling, with white braids piled up on top of her head. My first impression was of her strength. She touched my face with her strong, wrinkled hands, and I felt more than saw the deep compassion in her eyes. I looked around her studiolike room, which had a high ceiling and white adobe walls. Everything was very simple. On the wall hung a beautiful tapestry of muted tones that she had woven on her loom. She showed me translucent, paper-thin ceramic containers that she had just fired. They glowed. She was reclaiming an ancient alchemical process. They were as fragile as eggshells, delicate yet sturdy, like the balance we all must learn to walk in life. She held me close and told me that there was still much work to be done. She showed me many circles of people waiting outside. They rippled out like rings of water in a pond after a pebble has been cast. As I left, she put a small white stone in my hand. I still felt her hand on my cheek when I returned.

Finally, if it is indeed true that we teach what it is we need to learn, then I still need to center myself, relax my body, quiet my mind from the distractions of day-to-day living, take myself less seriously, and go deeper into the realm of wisdom and universal knowings where there is hope, harmony, and cosmic unity. This is just the beginning. Remember that we teach who we are, and as we do these exercises with our children, students, families, and other adults, we all become as children, reclaiming the wonder, the mystery, and joy of it all.

EXERCISE 29
Wave

AGE: 5 through adult
TIME: 5 minutes

As you breathe in . . . and . . . out, imagine that you are on a wave on the sea going up . . . and . . . down . . . up . . . and down. You are perfectly safe, either lying on your back in the water, lying on a raft or surfboard, or sitting in a sailboat being gently rocked by the motion of the sea. And as you continue to move up . . . and . . . down . . . back . . . and . . . forth, you will notice the warmth of the sun relaxing you and feel a gentle ocean breeze. You may notice the color of the sky, the smell of the sea air, and the sound of sea birds above. You notice a sense of calm throughout your entire body as you experience the gentle rocking motion of the sea. Allow yourself to feel nurtured and supported. (*Pause 1 minute*)

Now it is time to come back. I will count to three, and when you are ready, slowly open your eyes. One . . . two . . . three.

EXERCISE 30

Sanctuary

AGE: 15 through adult
EXERCISE: 10 minutes
FOLLOW-UP: 15 minutes

Close your eyes and begin to focus your attention on your breath, watching the air move in and out of your nostrils. Give yourself the suggestion that with each exhalation your body becomes more and more relaxed. (*Pause*) Good. Now imagine that you are moving through time and space to a place that is a sanctuary for you. The sanctuary is safe, simple, and beautiful. It may be located in nature, in the hills or near the sea, it may be in your room at home, or any place of your own choosing where you feel safe and secure. Go there now and experience the colors, textures, smells, sounds, tastes, and how your body feels in this place. You'll have several minutes of clock time equal to all the time you need to relax in this sanctuary. (*Pause for 3 minutes*)

Now it is time to return here, bringing with you the sense of safety and security that you have experienced in your sanctuary, ready to draw it or write about it. In a moment, I will count to five. Open your eyes at the count of five, feeling relaxed and alert. One . . . two . . . three . . . four . . . five.

NOTE: During this imagery exercise you may wish to play either *Sojourn: Music of the Spirit for Piano and Orchestra* or *Gymnosphere of the Rose*.

RESPONSE TO SANCTUARY EXERCISE

My sanctuary is an enclosed clearing, surrounded by palms and other green plants. A stream runs through; large stones make a resting place by the stream. It is silent but for the sound of birds and the sound of the stream. A small stone pagoda lies across the stream from the resting place. My ally, the fox, lies beside me on his side. A cool breeze runs through. The blue sky is visible, with some white, billowy, clear clouds above the opening at the top of the trees. It seems like the perfect fusion of nature and man-made garden.—*Matt, age eighteen*

NOTE TO PARENTS

Exercise 31 may initiate a discussion about a child's birth and who attended that birth. Focus on your excitement about the birth of your child instead of the details about the difficulty of the birthing process. Some children and adolescents will have an accurate memory of their birth and will remember relatives or neighbors who were there to welcome their arrival home.

NOTE TO TEACHERS

This is a good exercise to do with seniors in high school who are starting to address the issue of separation from their parents and the school community. In the imagery exercise they may experience bonding with a parent, grandparent, relative, or friend whom they have not seen in many years. Many emotions may be released. They feel how special they were as a newborn and can begin to talk about their fears and expectations of a life separate from their parents and friends as they move on to college or work. They may also get a sense of their own potential and what they want to do with their lives.

EXERCISE 31
Knowing Your Potential

AGE: 17 through adult
EXERCISE: 10 minutes
FOLLOW-UP: 15–20 minutes

Close your eyes and begin to focus your attention on your breath. Notice the air going in and out of your nostrils. Give yourself the suggestion that with each exhalation your body becomes more and more relaxed. Good. Today we are going to travel back in time (seventeen or eighteen years) to the time right after your birth. Your parents have brought you home, and you are lying in your bassinet, cradle, or crib, listening to the voices of loved ones around you. They are very happy that you are here; they have waited a long time for your birth. You feel yourself as a small infant with smooth skin and tiny hands and feet, noticing the colors, shapes, and sounds around you. Someone—it may be your mother, father, grandparent, or a friend—reaches over and gently lifts you up, supporting your head and body. This person holds you close, and you feel secure, supported, and nurtured. This person begins to tell you how much he or she loves you and welcomes you into this life. As you listen, you feel loved and you become aware of your potential in this lifetime. You have three minutes of clock time equal to all of the time you need to listen to this person, to feel his or her support, and to know your own potential. Begin. (*Pause 3 minutes*)

Now gently leave that image and come back in time to your present age. Bring with you the recognition of who you are and the feeling of love and support that you experienced. I will count to ten. Join me at the count of six, opening your eyes at ten, feeling relaxed and alert. One . . . two . . . three . . . four . . . five . . . six . . . seven . . . eight . . . nine . . . ten.

The Inner Child and The Extended Self[2]

Know that it is true that deep inside you there still exists a little girl or boy who is not aware that she or he has grown up. Also know that there lives within you your extended self, the self that has reached its full potential, your wise woman or wise man. In the following exercises you will contact both your child and your extended being, learning from the curiosity and wonder of the child and the wisdom and knowledge of the elder. You will have the opportunity to befriend your child in a way that may heal any patterns or disabling behavior that you actually learned in your childhood.

◎ _____

NOTE TO PARENTS AND TEACHERS

Give adolescents 10–15 minutes to draw or write about Exercise 32 before discussing it. They may experience a variety of emotions—sadness or happiness for the little girl or boy they have left behind, recollections of freedom, delight and curiosity, or a longing to be young again. For some a real healing may occur if they have been able to support the inner child. Spend as much time as is comfortable discussing their experiences before moving on to the next part of this exercise. Time limitations may require that you lead the next part of the exercise at another sitting.

◎ _____

EXERCISE 32
The Inner Child

AGE: 15 through adult
EXERCISE: 10–15 minutes
FOLLOW-UP: 15 minutes

Close your eyes and begin to follow your breath in and out of your nostrils. As you follow the movement of your breath, allow your body to relax. With each exhalation your body becomes more and more relaxed. Now prepare yourself to greet your child when she (or he) appears. She may be five, eight, or ten or whatever age is appropriate at this time. She may also change from age to age during her visit. Open your dominant hand (the hand that you write with) to hold the hand of your little girl (boy) when she arrives and feel the texture of her hand in yours. During the next several moments your child will appear. Begin to interact with her when she comes forth, letting her take the lead. Be the older friend of your child that she always wanted. If she wishes to take you to her secret hiding place or to the zoo or to her room to play with her, go there with her. She may wish to talk with you or may ask you to hold her. Be attentive to her needs and wants, and learn what she has to teach you. You'll have five minutes of clock time equal to all the time that you need to spend with your child. Begin. (*Pause 5 minutes*)

It is now time to say goodbye for the present. Thank your child for the time you have spent together, and tell her that you will call upon her to return again soon. (*Pause*)

In a moment I will count to ten. Join me at the count of six, opening your eyes at ten, feeling relaxed and alert and ready to record your visit with your child. One . . . two . . . three . . . four . . . five . . . six . . . seven . . . eight . . . nine . . . ten.

NOTE TO PARENTS AND TEACHERS

Give adolescents 10–15 minutes to draw or write about Exercise 33 and then discuss it. Many adolescents are surprised by the vivid image of their extended self, feel renewed by it, and continue to call upon this "wise being" in times of confusion or when making important decisions.

EXERCISE 33

The Extended Self

AGE: 15 through adult
EXERCISE: 10–15 minutes
FOLLOW-UP: 15 minutes

Close your eyes and begin to follow your breath in and out of your nostrils. Now give yourself the suggestion that with each exhalation your body becomes more and more relaxed. In this exercise you will call forth from the future your extended self, the you that has reached his (her) full potential and wisdom. Once again, open your dominant hand to receive the hand of your wise being. Feel the texture of his skin. When he appears, begin to interact with him, learning from his life experience and wisdom. Notice the environments he shows you, the colors, sounds, smells, and tastes. You will have five minutes of clock time equal to all of the time you need to be with your extended self. Begin. (*Pause 5 minutes*)

Now bring your extended self to meet your little child. The three of you sit down together; your extended self is holding you, and you are holding your child. Feel the union of the three, the love and wisdom and power of all aspects of your self. (*Pause 1 minute*)

Now release both your child and extended self into their time/space dimension, knowing that you can call upon them again and that they will always be there for you. (*Pause*)

Now become aware of who you are in your wholeness. In a moment I will count to ten. Join me at the count of six, opening your eyes at ten, feeling relaxed and alert and ready to record your experience.

Notes

One: A New Look at Our Children

1. Peter Russell, *The Brain Book* (New York: Hawthorne Books, 1979), p. 56.
2. Michael Grady and E. Lueche, *Education and the Brain* (Phi Delta Kappa, Educational Foundation, 1978).
3. Russell, p. 159.
4. Jean Houston, "Consider the Stradivarius," *Dromenon* 1, no. 5–6 (February 1979), p. 41.
5. Russell, p. 133.

Four: Learning with All the Senses

1. See Richard Bandler and John Grinder, *Frogs into Princes: Neurolinguistic Programming* (Moab, Utah: Real People Press, 1979).
2. This exercise is adapted for children from an exercise by Jean Houston entitled "Left Brain, Right Brain" in Robert Masters and Jean Houston, *Listening to the Body: The Psychophysical Way to Health and Awareness* (New York: Delacorte, 1978), p. 169.
3. This exercise is adapted for children from an exercise by Jean Houston entitled "Cleansing the Rooms of Perception," used in "New Ways of Being" introductory workshops. For more information on Dr. Houston's work, write to Box 600, New York, NY 10970.

Five: Verbal versus Nonverbal Learning

1. Victor Goertzel and Mildred G. Goertzel, *Cradles of Eminence* (Boston: Little, Brown, 1962), p. 251.

Six: Improving Skills through Imagery

1. Quoted in Sheila Ostrander and Lynn Schroeder, *Superlearning* (New York: Delacorte, 1979), p. 159.
2. Ibid., p. 158.

3. This exercise is adapted for children from an exercise by Jean Houston used in her "New Ways of Being" introductory workshops.
4. Ibid.

Seven: Making Self-Expression Easy

1. *New Strategies in Indian Education: Utilizing the Indian Child's Advantages in the Elementary Classroom.* Ministry of Education, Special Education Division, Indian Education Branch, Province of British Columbia, Canada, February 2–20, 1981.

Eight: A Positive Self-Image

1. *Year End Report: Awareness and Communication throughout the School,* an ESEA IV-C Project, Los Angeles City Schools, 1981–1982. On file with the Center for Integrative Learning, 450 West End Avenue, #14B, New York, NY 10024.
2. *Year End Report: Confluent Language Program for K–3 NES/LES Students,* an ESEA IV-C Project, Los Angeles City Schools, 1978–1981. On file with the Center for Integrative Learning (see note 1).
3. Maureen H. Murdock, "Meditation with Young Children," *Journal of Transpersonal Psychology* 10, no. 1 (1978): 39.
4. Exercises 18 and 19 are adapted from Jean Houston's exercise "Mea Machina/Mea Mandala" in *Life Force: The Psycho-Historical Recovery of the Self* (New York: Dell, 1980), pp. 172–178.

Nine: Inner and Outer Harmony

1. Lawrence LeShan, *How to Meditate: A Guide to Self-Discovery* (Boston: Little, Brown, 1974), p. 37.
2. Center for Attitudinal Healing, *There Is a Rainbow Behind Every Dark Cloud* (Millbrae, Calif.: Celestial Arts, 1978), p. 63.
3. Paul D. MacLean, M.D., "A Mind of Three Minds: Educating the Triune Brain," in *Education and the Brain* (Chicago: National Society for the Study of Education, 1978), p. 340.
4. This exercise is adapted for children from an exercise entitled "Heart Meditation" in Bernard Gunther, *Energy, Ecstasy* (Los Angeles: Guild of Tutors Press, 1978), p. 62.

Ten: Entering Adolescence

1. Abraham H. Maslow, *Toward a Psychology of Being* (New York: Van Nostrand Reinhold, 1968), pp. 199–200.
2. Eugene T. Gendlin, *Focusing* (New York: Bantam Books, 1978), p. 10.
3. Herman T. Epstein, "Growth Spurts during Brain Development," *NSSE Yearbook,* part 2 (1978), pp. 343–370.
4. Adapted from the focusing work of Eugene T. Gendlin.

Eleven: The Quest for Identity

1. Diana Whitmore, *Psychosynthesis in Education* (Rochester, Vt.: Destiny Books, 1986), p. 151.
2. Exercises 32 and 33 are adapted for adolescents from exercises by Jean Houston used in her "New Ways of Being" introductory workshops.

Bibliography

In addition to the books and articles listed in the Notes section, the following sources have made an invaluable contribution to the writing of this book.

BOOKS

Argüelles, José and Miriam. *Mandala.* Berkeley: Shambhala Publications, Inc. 1972.

Bell, Ruth, and Leni Zeiger Wildflower. *Changing Bodies, Changing Lives.* New York: Random House, 1980.

————. *Talking with Your Teenager: A Book for Parents.* New York: Random House, 1983.

Buzan, Tony. *Use Both Sides of Your Brain.* New York: E.P. Dutton & Co., 1976.

Feild, Reshad. *The Last Barrier.* New York: Harper & Row, 1976.

Feldenkrais, M. *Awareness through Movement: Health Exercises for Personal Growth.* New York: Harper & Row, 1972.

Galyean, Beverly-Colleene. *Mind Sight: Learning through Imaging.* Long Beach, Calif.: Center for Integrative Learning, 1983. Available by writing to Center for Integrative Learning, 450 West End Avenue, #14B, New York, NY 10024.

Gardner, Howard. *Frames of Mind: The Theory of Multiple Intelligences.* New York: Basic Books, 1983.

Goertzel, Victor, and Mildred G. Goertzel. *Cradles of Eminence.* Boston: Little, Brown, 1962.

Hampden-Turner, Charles. *Maps of the Mind.* New York: Collier Books, 1981.

Hendricks, Gay, and Thomas B. Roberts. *The Second Centering Book: More Awareness Activities for Children, Parents and Teachers.* Englewood Cliffs, N.J.: Prentice-Hall, 1977.

Kazantzakis, Nikos. *Zorba the Greek.* New York: Simon & Schuster, 1952.

Leonard, George. *The Silent Pulse.* New York: E. P. Dutton, 1978.

Machado, Luis Alberto. *The Right to Be Intelligent.* New York: Pergamon Press, 1980.

Maslow, Abraham H. *Religions, Values and Peak-Experiences.* New York: Penguin Books, 1970.

Masters, Robert, and Jean Houston. *Listening to the Body: The Psychophysical Way to Health and Awareness.* New York: Delacorte, 1978.

————. *Mind Games: The Guide to Inner Space.* New York: Dell, 1973.

Pearce, Joseph Chilton. *The Crack in the Cosmic Egg.* New York: Washington Square Press, 1973.

———. *Magical Child.* New York: Bantam, 1980.

———. *Magical Child Matures.* New York: Dutton, 1985.

Pietsch, Paul. *Shufflebrain: The Quest for the Holographic Mind.* Boston: Houghton Mifflin Co., 1981.

Restak, Richard M. *The Brain: The Last Frontier.* New York: Warner Books, 1979.

Rozman, Deborah. *Meditation for Children.* Millbrae, Calif.: Celestial Arts, 1976.

———. *Meditating with Children.* Boulder Creek, Calif.: University of the Trees Press, 1975.

Sagan, Carl. *The Dragons of Eden.* New York: Random House, 1977.

Samples, Bob. *Mind of Our Mother.* Reading, Mass.: Addison-Wesley Publishing, 1981.

Sendak, Maurice. *Where the Wild Things Are.* New York: Penguin Books, 1963.

Steiner, Rudolf. *Soul Economy and Waldorf Education.* New York: Anthroposophic Press, 1986.

Tobias, Sheila. *Overcoming Math Anxiety.* Boston: Houghton Mifflin Co., 1978.

Periodicals

Brain/Mind Bulletin, P.O. Box 42211, 4717 N. Figueroa Street, Los Angeles, CA 90042.

Journal of Humanistic Psychology, 325 Ninth Street, San Francisco, CA 94103.

Journal of Transpersonal Psychology, P.O. Box 4437, Stanford, CA 94305.

On the Beam, New Horizons for Learning, P.O. Box 51140, Seattle, WA 98115.

Suggested Recordings

These recordings can be played as background music for imagery exercises.

Callings, Paul Winter, Living Music Foundation, Box 68, Litchfield, CT 06759.

Canon in D, Pachelbel, RCA Victrola, VICS-1687.

Caverna Magica, Andreas Vollenweider, CBS, 1983.

The Changer and the Changed, Chris Williamson, Olivia Records, 4400 Market Street, Oakland, CA 94608.

Chariots of Fire, Vangelis, Polydor PD-1-6335.

Deep Breakfast, Ray Lynch, Ray Lynch Productions, 1984.

Environment Series on the Atlantic Label (Syntonic Research Series): sounds of nature—birds, seashore, countryside, rain, thunderstorms, etc.

The Four Seasons, Vivaldi, Angel S-37053 with Itzak Perlman.

Golden Voyage, Ron Dexter, Awakening Productions, 4132 Tuller Avenue, Culver City, CA 90230.

Gymnosphere: Song of the Rose, Jordon de la Sierra, Unity Records, Box 12 Corte Madera, CA 94925.

Heaven and Hell, Vangelis, RCA LPL-1-5110.

Ignacio, Vangelis, Egg Records (900.531) P-1977 Pema Music, Distribution C.P.F.

India, Kitaro, Griffin Recording. Produced by Takananri for Sound Design Inc., Warner Bros., Inc., 1985.

Inside II, Paul Horn, EPIC KE 31600.

Millennia, Kitaro, Sound Design.

The Moldau, Smetana, George Szell, Columbia Stereo Y30049.

Music for Zen Meditation and Other Joys, Verve V6-8634.

Oxygene, Jean-Michel Jarre, Polydor PD-1-6112.

Passages, William Ackerman, Windham Hill Records.

Pianoscapes, Michel Jones, 28 Carey Road, Toronto, Ontario M3H 3B3.

Reflections, Alan Stivell, Fontana.

Renaissance of the Celtic Harp, Alan Stivell, Applause by Phillips.

Sakura, music for flute and harp based on Japanese melodies, Jean-Pierre Rampal and Lily Laskine on Columbia M-34568.

Sky of Mind, Ray Lynch, Ray Lynch Productions, 1984.

Sojourn: Music of the Spirit for Piano and Orchestra, Search for Serenity, 180 W. 25 Street, Upland, CA. 91786-1113.

Spectrum Suite and *Ancient Echoes,* Steve Halpern, Spectrum Research Institute, 620 Taylor Way, #14, Belmont, CA 94002.

The Way In Is the Way Out, Marti Glenn and Leslie Spilsbury, Visionary Press, 7321 Lowell Way, Goleta, CA 93117.